Everything Is Bullshit

Priceonomics

For information, please contact us:
info@priceonomics.com

ISBN-10: 0692224963
ISBN-13: 978-0692224960

Priceonomics Authors
Zachary Crockett
Rohin Dhar
Alex Mayyasi

Special Contributor
David Raether

Cover Design
Dan Abramson

CONTENTS

INTRODUCTION:
THE BIG LIE

Which lies are so big that no one questions them?

In life, we grow up, attend school, get a job, buy a car, start a family, get a mortgage, lose a job, get a divorce, find a new job, start a new family, move a few times, retire, un-retire, re-retire, play some golf, and then die. Is it possible that as we act out this script, we occasionally make a very important life decision incorrectly because we had some misinformation? Almost certainly.

Misinformation has consequences. You could merely overpay for a bottle of wine. Or worse, you could waste tens of thousands of dollars and years of your life on the wrong kind of education. Or perhaps you'll spend much of your youth feeling bad about your body if you start to believe an advertising campaign. And sometimes when many people believe a particularly vicious lie, truly horrific things can happen.

The History of the Big Lie

The canonical example of a "Big Lie" in the 20th century is Adolf Hitler's propaganda machine. Hitler created a lie so reprehensible that it seemed impossible that the head of a government could simply make it up:

he claimed that Jews were responsible for all of Germany's problems.

Hitler's big lie led to the mass murder of millions of Jews, the slaughter of other minority groups, and a world-wide war. Today it seems unfathomable that such a blatant lie could instigate something so atrocious. But a mere 75 years ago, an entire nation committed an act of unthinkable evil in the service of a lie.

The term "big lie" was popularized by Hitler himself. In his 1925 autobiography *Mein Kampf*, Hitler wrote "that in the big lie there is always a certain force of credibility" because the public "would not believe that others could have the impudence to distort the truth so infamously." Hitler painted Germany's Jews as perpetrators of the big lie, scapegoating them for the country's defeat in World War I. Even in coining the phrase "big lie," Hitler did so with a big lie.

. After World War II, the United States military produced an anti-communist film called "The Big Lie," which began with the Hitler quote: "The great masses will more easily fall victim to a big lie than to a small one." The film likened Hitler to Stalin, Nazis to Communists, and World War II to the struggle against Communism. The strength of big lies is that simple, forceful statements seem true. Selling the American public on the formula that Communists are the new Nazis was an easier justification for the Cold War than the complicated reality of communist revolutions intertwining with geopolitics, anti-colonial movements, and nationalist sentiments. A big lie sidesteps the need for a debate about the facts.

In 2003, the United States government invaded Iraq based on evidence that Saddam Hussein had weapons of mass destruction. But the weapons didn't exist; instead, politicians jumped to a conclusion that the data did not actually support. Who could believe that the American government would be impudent enough to start a war over flimsy data?

Governments perpetrate some of the most consequential big lies. Sometimes the lying is overt. Other times, leaders selectively weigh evidence to draw their preferred conclusions. Either way is lying.

But big lies have other progenitors. Once you start looking for big lies, you'll find the world is built on many ideas that the facts don't necessarily support. Yet we accept them because "that's just the way things are."

The Marketing of a Big Lie

For us, the revelation of the power of a big lie came when we investigated the history of diamond engagement rings. Our whole lives, we've been inculcated with the notion that diamonds are valuable and wonderful. Diamonds are "a girl's best friend," priceless family heirlooms, and the best way to express your love. To get married, a man has to buy a diamond engagement ring and spend approximately two months' salary on the purchase.

Why two months' salary? Why diamonds? As it turns it, the tradition of proposing with diamond engagement rings is largely a 20th century marketing invention by De Beers, a company that has a global monopoly on the diamond supply. If a fundamental part of American life is a marketing gimmick to drum up demand for diamonds, what else out there is bullshit?

So the Priceonomics team started researching things that seemed suspicious to us. Why is wine so expensive? Why is it harder for Asians to get into Harvard than other students? How does art become "art"? Why does college cost so much? Why do college football and basketball coaches make so much money while players are unpaid? Why do so many pets die in animal shelters?

Why is the world the way it is, and which practices

fall apart under scrutiny? The result is this book.

***

In our view, the big lie of our society is the notion that our current beliefs and traditions are based on solid facts. When you start investigating some of our most hallowed values, you find that much of what we hold dear is actually based on historical accident, the profit motives of a few companies, or the agenda of someone who died long ago. A lot of what we believe and do is bullshit, yet we walk around thinking that it's objectively the right way of doing things.

The philosophy of this book is that the best defense against a big lie is curiosity. How did a particular custom originate, and who benefits from its existence? This line of questioning can lead you down an illuminating and sometimes disturbing rabbit hole. It can also allow you to identify and call attention to practices you believe need to change.

The title *Everything is Bullshit* may sound cynical, but we see it differently. If so much of what we believe is bullshit, that means that many of our social values are up for grabs to be influenced. On one hand, it's scary to think that some of our most cherished traditions were implanted by others to serve their own purposes. On the other hand, it's liberating to know that you can actually impact the values that people hold dear.

You have the option to build the next generation of companies, institutions, and ideas. If you think companies are misbehaving, you can start a campaign that shames them publicly. If you're disappointed that the government is spying on us, you can work on the technology to make that more difficult. If you think police brutality is out of hand, you can make it easier for citizens to record and share when these violations take place. If you think we live in a sexist world, you can start a movement that helps change how people think about sex, gender and our bodies.

Everything we believe today is the result of a movement someone else started long ago. You can shape the future version of the world, just as others shaped the current one.

If you see something out there that is bullshit, you can replace it with something that is not.

PRICEONOMICS

PART I:
STATUS SYMBOLS

"What is a cynic? A man who knows the price of everything and the value of nothing."

(Oscar Wilde, *Lady Windermere's Fan*)

PRICEONOMICS

1.

DIAMONDS ARE BULLSHIT

American males enter adulthood through a peculiar rite of passage: they spend most of their savings on a shiny piece of rock. They could invest the money in assets that will compound over time and someday provide a nest egg. Instead, they trade that money for a diamond ring, which isn't much of an asset at all. As soon as a diamond leaves a jeweler, it loses over 50% of its value.

We exchange diamond rings as part of the engagement process because the diamond company De Beers decided in 1938 that it would like us to. Prior to a stunningly successful marketing campaign, Americans occasionally exchanged engagement rings, but it wasn't pervasive. Not only is the demand for diamonds a marketing invention, but diamonds aren't actually that rare. Only by carefully restricting the supply has De Beers kept the price of a diamond high.

Countless American dudes will attest that the societal obligation to furnish a diamond engagement ring is both stressful and expensive. But this obligation only exists because the company that stands to profit from it willed it into existence.

So here is a modest proposal: Let's agree that diamonds are bullshit and reject their role in the marriage process. Let's admit that we as a society were tricked for about a century into coveting sparkling pieces of carbon, but it's time to end the nonsense.

The Concept of Intrinsic Value

In finance, there is concept called intrinsic value. An asset's value is essentially driven by the (discounted) value of the future cash that asset will generate. For example, when Hertz buys a car, its value is the profit Hertz will earn from renting it out and selling the car at the end of its life (the "terminal value"). For Hertz, a car is an investment. When you buy a car, unless you make money from it somehow, its value corresponds to its resale value. Since a car is a depreciating asset, the amount of value that the car loses over its lifetime is a very real expense you pay.

A diamond is a depreciating asset masquerading as an investment. There is a common misconception that jewelry and precious metals are assets that can store value, appreciate, and hedge against inflation. That's not wholly untrue.

Gold and silver are commodities that can be purchased on financial markets. They can appreciate and hold value in times of inflation. You can even hoard gold under your bed and buy gold coins and bullion (albeit at approximately a 10% premium to market rates). If you want to hoard gold jewelry, however, there is typically a 100-400% retail markup. So jewelry is not a wise investment.

But with that caveat in mind, the market for gold is fairly liquid and gold is fungible — you can trade one large piece of gold for ten smalls ones like you can trade a ten dollar bill for ten one dollar bills. These characteristics make it a feasible investment.

Diamonds, however, are not an investment. The

market for them is not liquid, and diamonds are not fungible.

The first test of a liquid market is whether you can resell a diamond. In a famous piece published by The Atlantic in 1982, Edward Epstein explains why you can't sell used diamonds for anything but a pittance:

> *"Retail jewelers, especially the prestigious Fifth Avenue stores, prefer not to buy back diamonds from customers, because the offer they would make would most likely be considered ridiculously low. The 'keystone,' or markup, on a diamond and its setting may range from 100 to 200 percent, depending on the policy of the store; if it bought diamonds back from customers, it would have to buy them back at wholesale prices.*
>
> *Most jewelers would prefer not to make a customer an offer that might be deemed insulting and also might undercut the widely held notion that diamonds go up in value. Moreover, since retailers generally receive their diamonds from wholesalers on consignment, and need not pay for them until they are sold, they would not readily risk their own cash to buy diamonds from customers."*

When you buy a diamond, you buy it at retail, which is a 100% to 200% markup. If you want to resell it, you have to pay less than wholesale to incent a diamond buyer to risk her own capital on the purchase. Given the large markup, this will mean a substantial loss on your part. The same article puts some numbers around the dilemma:

> *"Because of the steep markup on diamonds, individuals who buy retail and in effect sell wholesale often suffer enormous losses. For example, Brod estimates that a half-carat diamond ring, which might cost $2,000 at a retail jewelry store, could be sold for only $600 at Empire."*

Some diamonds are perhaps investment grade, but you probably don't own one, even if you spent a lot. Empire Diamonds estimates that only one in several thousand of the diamonds it appraises are actually of investment grade quality.

The diamond classification scheme is extremely complicated, and as a result, diamonds are not fungible and can't be easily exchanged with each other. Diamond professionals use the 4 C's when classifying and pricing diamonds: carats, color, cut, and clarity. Due to the complexity of these 4 dimensions, it's hard to make apples to apples comparisons between diamonds.

But even when looking at the value of one stone, professionals seem like they're just making up diamond prices. In 1977, a jewelry industry magazine asked a number of dealers to value a diamond; their valuations varied by over 100%.

So let's be very clear, a diamond is not an investment. You might want one because it looks pretty or to have a "massive rock", but not because it will store value or appreciate in value.

But among all the pretty, shiny things out there — gold and silver, rubies and emeralds — why do Americans covet diamond engagement rings?

A Diamond is a Measure of Manhood

"The reason you haven't felt it is because it doesn't exist. What you call love was invented by guys like me, to sell nylons."
(Don Draper, Madmen)

We like diamonds because Gerold M. Lauck told us to. Until the mid 20th century, diamond engagement rings were a small and dying industry in America, and the concept had not really taken hold in Europe.

Not surprisingly, the American market for diamond engagement rings began to shrink during the Great Depression. Sales volume declined and the buyers that remained purchased increasingly smaller stones. But the U.S. market for engagement rings was still 75% of De Beers' sales. With Europe on the verge of war, it didn't seem like a promising place to invest. If De Beers was going to grow, it had to reverse the trend.

And so, in 1938, De Beers turned to Madison Avenue for help. The company hired Gerold Lauck and the N. W. Ayer advertising agency, which commissioned a study with some astute observations. Namely, men were the key to the market. As Epstein wrote of the findings:

> *"Since 'young men buy over 90% of all engagement rings' it would be crucial to inculcate in them the idea that diamonds were a gift of love: the larger and finer the diamond, the greater the expression of love. Similarly, young women had to be encouraged to view diamonds as an integral part of any romantic courtship."*

However, there was a dilemma. Many smart and prosperous women didn't want diamond engagement rings. They wanted to be different.

> *"The millions of brides and brides-to-be are subjected to at least two important pressures that work against the diamond engagement ring. Among the more prosperous, there is the sophisticated urge to be different as a means of being smart.... the lower-income groups would like to show more for the money than they can find in the diamond they can afford..."*

Lauck needed to sell a product that people either did not want or could not afford. His solution would haunt men for generations. He advised that De Beers market diamonds as a status symbol:

> *"The substantial diamond gift can be made a more widely sought symbol of personal and family success — an expression of socio-economic achievement. Promote the diamond as one material object which can reflect, in a very personal way, a man's ... success in life."*

***

The next time you look at a diamond, consider this: nearly every American marriage begins with a diamond because a bunch of rich white men in the 1940s convinced everyone that its size determines a man's self worth. They created this convention — that unless a man purchases (an intrinsically useless) diamond, his life is a failure — while sitting in a room, racking their brains on how to sell diamonds that no one wanted.

With this insight, they began marketing diamonds as a symbol of status and love. Epstein documents the campaign in his article for The Atlantic:

> *"Movie idols, the paragons of romance for the mass audience, would be given diamonds to use as their symbols of indestructible love. In addition, the agency suggested offering stories and society photographs to selected magazines and newspapers which would reinforce the link between diamonds and romance. Stories would stress the size of diamonds that celebrities presented to their loved ones, and photographs would conspicuously show the glittering stone on the hand of a well-known woman.*
>
> *Fashion designers would talk on radio programs about the "trend towards diamonds" that Ayer planned to start. The Ayer plan also envisioned using the British royal family to help foster the romantic allure of diamonds."*

Even the royal family was in on the hoax. The campaign paid immediate dividends. Within 3 years, despite the Great Depression, diamond sales in the U.S. increased 55%. Twenty years later, an entire generation believed that an expensive diamond ring was a necessary step in the marriage process.

The De Beers marketing machine continued to churn out the hits. It circulated marketing materials suggesting, apropos of nothing, that a man should spend one month's salary on a diamond ring. It worked so well that De Beers arbitrarily decided to increase the suggestion to two months' salary. That's why people think that they need to spend two months' salary on a ring — because the suppliers of the product said so.

Today, over 80% of women in the U.S. receive diamond rings when they get engaged. The domination is complete.

A History of Market Manipulation

What, you might ask, could top institutionalizing demand for a useless product out of thin air? Monopolizing the supply of diamonds for over a century to make that useless product extremely expensive. You see, diamonds aren't really even that rare.

Before 1870, diamonds were very rare. They typically ended up in a Maharaja's crown or a royal necklace. In 1870, enormous deposits of diamonds were discovered in Kimberley, South Africa. As diamonds flooded the market, the financiers of the mines realized they were making their own investments worthless. As they mined more and more diamonds, they became less scarce and their price dropped.

The diamond market may have bottomed out were it not for an enterprising individual by the name of Cecil Rhodes. He began buying up mines in order to control the output and keep the price of diamonds high. By 1888, Rhodes controlled the entire South African diamond supply, and in turn, essentially the entire world supply. One of the companies he acquired was eponymously named after its founders, the De Beers brothers.

Building a diamond monopoly isn't easy work. It requires a balance of ruthlessly punishing and cooperating with competitors, as well as a very long term view. For example, in 1902, prospectors discovered a massive mine in South Africa that contained as many diamonds as all of De Beers' mines combined. The owners initially refused to join the De Beers cartel, and only joined three years later after new owner Ernest Oppenheimer recognized that a competitive market for diamonds would be disastrous for the industry. In Oppenheimer's words:

> *"Common sense tells us that the only way to increase the value of diamonds is to make them scarce, that is to reduce production."*

Here's how De Beers has controlled the diamond supply chain for most of the last century. De Beers owns most of the diamond mines. When faced with mines it doesn't own, De Beers has historically bought out all the diamonds, intimidating or co-opting any that think of resisting its monopoly. It then transfers all the diamonds over to the Central Selling Organization (CSO), which De Beers owns.

The CSO sorts through the diamonds, puts them in boxes and presents them to the 250 partners that it sells to. The price and quantity of the diamonds are non-negotiable — it's take it or leave it. Refuse your boxes and you're out of the diamond industry.

For most of the 20th century, this system controlled 90% of the diamond trade and was solely responsible for the inflated price of diamonds. As Oppenheimer took over leadership at De Beers, however, he keenly assessed the primary operational risk that the company faced:

> *"Our only risk is the sudden discovery of new mines, which human nature will work recklessly to the detriment of us all."*

Because diamonds are "valuable", there will always be the risk of entrepreneurs finding new sources of diamonds. Exercising control over new mines also often meant working with communists. In 1957, the Soviet Union discovered a massive deposit of diamonds in Siberia. Though the diamonds were a bit on the smallish side, De Beers still had to swoop in and buy all of them from the Soviets, lest it risk the supply being unleashed on the world market.

Later, in Australia, a large supply of colored diamonds was discovered. When the mine refused to join the syndicate, De Beers retaliated by unloading massive amounts of colored diamonds that were similar to the Australian ones to drive down their price. Similarly, in the 1970s, some Israeli members of the CSO started stockpiling the diamonds they were allocated rather than reselling them. This made it difficult for De Beers to control the market price and would eventually cause a deflation in diamond prices when the hoarders released their stockpile. Eventually, these offending members were banned from the CSO, essentially shutting them out from the diamond business.

In 2000, De Beers announced that it was relinquishing its monopoly on the diamond business. It even settled a U.S. Antitrust lawsuit related to price fixing industrial diamonds to the tune of $10 million. (How generous! What is that, the price of one investment banker's engagement ring?)

Today, De Beers' hold on the industry supply chain has weakened. And yet, prices continue to rise as new deposits have not been found recently and demand for diamonds is increasing in India and China. For now, it's less necessary that the company monopolize the supply chain because its lie that a diamond is a proxy for a man's worth in life has infected the rest of the world.

A Parting Thought

*"I didn't get a bathroom door that looks like a wall
by being bad at business."*
(Jack Donaghy, 30 Rock)

We covet diamonds in America for a simple reason: the company that stands to profit from diamond sales decided that we should. De Beers' marketing campaign single handedly made diamond rings the measure of one's success in America. Despite diamonds' complete lack of inherent value, the company manufactured an image of diamonds as a status symbol. And to keep the price of diamonds high, despite the abundance of new diamond finds, De Beers executed the most effective monopoly of the 20th century. Okay, we get it De Beers, you guys are really good at business!

The purpose of this chapter is to point out that diamond engagement rings are a lie — they're an invention of Madison Avenue and De Beers. We have completely glossed over the sheer amount of human suffering that this lie has caused: conflict diamonds that fund wars, money that supported apartheid for decades, and the pillaging of the earth to find shiny carbon. And while we're on the subject, why is it that women need to be asked and presented with a ring in order to get married? Why can't they ask and do the presenting?

Diamonds are not actually scarce, make a terrible investment, and are purely valuable as a status symbol.

Diamonds, to put it delicately, are bullshit.

2.

THE SEAL CLUBBING BUSINESS

Every March, Richard Whelan boards the Shepherd II — one of hundreds of hunting vessels in Newfoundland, Canada — and drifts into the frigid eastern waters to hunt for seals. For two months, he lives aboard the battered ship, subsisting on minimal rations and braving blisteringly cold temperatures.

When Whelan spots a seal scooting across the ice, he takes out his .22 Magnum, high caliber rifle, zeroes in from a distance, and fires. In the ensuing moments, he docks the boat, chases the animal down and bashes in its skull with a taloned wooden club — a practice known as "seal clubbing." After ensuring the seal is dead, Whelan swiftly peels off its fur with a 12-inch knife; often, the majority of the animal's body is left behind on the blood-stained ice. Though channels exist for seal meat and oil, the animal's fur, which is processed, tanned, and fashioned into $4,000 luxury coats, is the sealer's crown jewel.

Despite the attention it receives, the seal industry is quite small today, though this wasn't always the case. During its golden age, sealing was the second largest source of revenue in Newfoundland's isolated economy; by last year, it accounted for less than 1%. Led by animal rights groups and celebrity supporters, decades-long anti-seal clubbing campaigns have severely crippled the trade. Seal products are now banned in nearly every market — the U.S., Japan, and the majority of Europe included — and strict regulations and quotas have been instituted by the Canadian government.

But seals are not one of the world's 20,000 endangered species, nor are they scarce in Canada. For most seal hunters, the dying hunting industry, worth only around $1.5 million in annual sales, is only a part-time job and provides little financial security.

Why did the world organize itself to effectively end the practice of seal clubbing — especially when there exists a plethora of threatened species that are slaughtered on larger scales? And while "clubbing" a seal with a mallet out in the wild sounds terrible, is that worse than killing an animal that lives the entirety of its life in a processing plant?

Could it be that we saved seals simply because they're cute?

The Birth of the Sealing Trade

Sealing has a rich, complex history. Though practiced in multiple cultures (Namibia, Greenland, Norway, Russia, Iceland), over 97% of seal hunting has historically occurred in Newfoundland and Labrador, on the eastern coast of Canada.

For Inuits and native peoples of Newfoundland, seal hunting dates back more than 4,000 years. In the harsh, icy territories, these animals provided a means of sustenance: meat — rich in fat, protein, and vitamins A and C — provided necessary nutrients; fur pelts were fashioned into coats, boots, and blankets. When a young Inuit boy killed his first seal, it would be cause for celebration: a huge feast would be held, and every part of the animal would be utilized.

By the early 16th century, an influx of Portuguese, French, British, and Basque settlers had established a commercial sealing industry. These men — most of whom were fishermen — would organize multi-month expeditions to earn extra income in the cod off-season. A significant seal market soon emerged in Europe, where the fur was valued for its warmth and oils were championed as a healing agent; by 1773, 128,000 seals were being harvested each year.

Sealing continued to grow, and in the 19th century, the trade saw its Golden Age. Foreign investors stepped in and the hunt greatly expanded, employing shipbuilders, carpenters, and refiners, who extracted oil from seal blubber and sold it as a dietary supplement. Between 1800 and 1900, over 33 million seals were harvested. Sealing became inextricably weaved into Newfoundland's economy, and trailed only cod fishing as the province's biggest revenue stream, pulling in $1.5 million per year ($28 million in 2014 dollars).

Large steam-powered vessels were introduced in the early 20th century, allowing for bigger hunts over wider territories, but not without risk: the ships were prone to accident, and in a 50 year span, 400 ships were lost and nearly 1,000 men perished. In one instance — The Great Newfoundland Sealing Disaster of 1914 — 78 sealers perished and another 173 were lost at sea, never to be found. Ships were controlled by wealthy investors, and employment conditions for sealers soon deteriorated: they were underfed (eating only biscuits and tea for days at a time), given little in the way of warm clothing and safety gear, and were allocated little time for sleep or rest.

During World War II, most sealing vessels were enlisted for use in the service, and the industry came to a stand-still; in the 1960s, it emerged with a vengeance, fueled by an incredible demand for newly-in-vogue fur.

With machinery, increased labor forces, and more scalable methods of production in place, annual seal kills rocketed to over 300,000 per year; for the first time in its history, the trade began to attract a pushback.

Years of regulation, lobbying, and anti-sealing campaigning ensued, and at the heart of the debate were the "seal clubbers" themselves.

The Life of a Modern-Day Sealer

For seal hunters registered in Canada, life isn't grand. The average harvester earns only 20-35% of his yearly income — a meager $5,000 to 8,000 — from sealing, and relies on other work to survive. A vast majority of sealers come from Canada's poorest, most isolated regions and have few alternatives for work.

For many years, William Case, a night watchman by trade, participated in the seal hunt to earn extra income. In an interview with the Canadian Geographical Society, he elucidates a lifestyle that is both incredibly difficult and non-lucrative. Docking a schooner in early March, he'd be at sea for two months with limited supplies, often facing great dangers and harsh terrain.

One time, sailing out in remote waters, Case's vessel came across a small rowboat that had drifted out to sea; inside were two men: one dead, and the other "with his arms frozen to his oars, and clinging to life." The life of a sealer, reminds Case, "ain't for the faint of heart." Undoubtedly, sealers face some of the harshest weather conditions in North America, braving the frigid eastern waters of Newfoundland. Leo Seymour, an ex-sealer, says that on a "rough year" like 2014, ice conditions can be nightmarish:

> *"It's wicked. It's wicked. Bad days. Blowing gales and then the fog and everything. And the ice is so heavy. I s'pose some*

fellers takes a chance on it. Some fellers might have 1,500 or a couple of thousand seals so it's not so bad. But if you're only getting a couple of hundred seals it's not even worth fueling up your boat for. You can't even pay your expense."

But sealing has harsher realities than the weather: animals must be clubbed to death. Case, whose ship would haul in "between 300 and 1,500 seals," recalls the "rather crude" method used to get the job done:

"When we could reach them on the ice cakes, a blow on the snout with a club would do the trick. We shot them in open water and fished them out with gaffs. Sometimes, you'd shoot one from a distance and trek about a mile or two. We went in small boats, two men in each one, the gunner and the other his mate. We skinned the seals on the ice. A rip with the knife and in a jiffy the pelt would be taken off and the carcass left for the birds. Sometimes, the old hoods [seals] would make at us, but we could dodge them, as they always moved along in a straight line, and then the club or the gun would soon fix them."

The skins (or pelts) are the means of financial sub-sistence for the hunters: while minimal markets exist for oil and meat, seal fur is the driving force of the in-dustry, constituting about 90% of the market. As such, sealers take great care to preserve them. Any knife knick or bullet hole in the pelt can result in price de-ductions when it comes time to sell them to processing plants and direct-contact kills are encouraged.

To slaughter a seal, a hunter uses a "hakapik," a heavy wooden club with a hammer head (used to crush the seal's skull) and a hook (used to drag away the carcass post-kill). The tool, a Norwegian innovation, is favored by sealers for its ability to make a supposedly "humane" kill without damaging the pelt.

Fergus Foley, who participated in the seal hunt for ten years to support his fishing income, says it can get a lot worse than clubbing a lone seal. Sometimes, pups, or baby seals, are lost in the process — something Foley's now immune to. In an interview with Canada's Department of Fisheries and Oceans, he clarifies some of the gruesome realities of his trade:

> *"The best day we done, we took approximately one hundred and eighty seals. I seen a female being pelted and the pup came out of her when they cut her open, the pup was dead. Someone passed the comment, 'If Greenpeace were only here to see this!' There were a few occasions when we took the female Hood seals and left the pup on the ice. On two occasions, I observed pups falling out of the female while being pelted on deck. The two pups I observed were alive and were thrown over the side. I seen these pups crawl up on the ice after we threw them over aboard."*

The Canadian Sealers' Association (the governing body that represents all of Canada's commercial seal hunters) maintains a strict set of "kill guidelines" that sealers must follow — both to ensure that fishery regulations are followed and to maximize profits from seal furs. In a "how-to" video intended for sealers, these methods are demonstrated. "The harvest must be based on sound science," the film warns, "humane killing is the key to success!"

According to the CSA's President, Frank Pinhorn, the humane way to go about killing a seal is a three-step process: "stun the seal with a swift knock to the head, check to ensure the skull is crushed, and cut him open to bleed out." Quality, reminds Pinhorn, is key here. A sealer must take great care not to "knick organs" during the skinning process, lest the skin, blubber, and meat be contaminated with byproducts ("bacteria spread from the gut can cost thousands of dollars").

The Seal Market: Making a $4,000 Coat

After furs are stripped from a seal, hunters return to the port and sell them "in raw form" to processing plants; blubber is removed and they are appropriately conditioned for use in clothing. These plants maintain a complex pricing system which encourages as little tampering with fur as possible and as much as $2 is deducted from each pelt for "knife knicks," yellowing (caused by excessive bleeding), and tears. The proper killing of a seal doesn't just benefit hunters, says Pinhorn — it "maximizes the financial benefit of all stakeholders involved in the industry."

But in reality, the payoff for hunters is minimal. Today, depending on quality, pelts go for $20-35 each; after the ship captain takes his cut, that amounts to a little over $15 for the hunter that clubbed the animal. Pelts are not particularly lucrative until the retail stage, and the process to get to that point is painstaking.

When processing plants purchase skins from sealing vessels, they come in crude form (bloody, and with blubber still attached). At the plant, the skins are soaked in brine for several weeks, then go through a tanning procedure; if a skin is excessively yellow or sun-spotted, it is typically dyed a dark color. From the plant, the pelts are sold to brokers, essentially middlemen with retail connections who sell them at a markup to clothing and accessory manufacturers. Once the goods are crafted, they are then disseminated to seal outerwear shops and sold for exorbitant prices.

***

Bernie Halloran operates Always in Vogue, one of several seal clothing stores in Newfoundland. After purchasing his skins directly from Carino (Canada's largest sealing plant), he acts as his own manufacturer in addition to retailing. Since Halloran is a long-time, local trader, he "receives special deals" on his wholesale fur purchases.

In Canada and other particularly frigid countries, seal fur doesn't just provide warmth — it serves as a status symbol. Halloran's shop carries an array of items: jackets, hats, bags, boots, and bow ties, and admits that his items (and seal products in general) are "classified as luxurious." A full-length seal coat parka made from "anthracite-colored top-tier fur" runs about $4,000; on the lower end, spotted seal throw pillows go for $150 a pop. When he first opened shop 30 years ago, Halloran enjoyed great business — until product bans and sealing backlash stampeded his success:

> "It is sad that the world markets have been slowly closing — Europe, USA, Russia. Seal is a bullied industry. What hypocrites! My thinking is right and I know it to be right...if killing seals is wrong, then the world is wrong. It's simple: if people don't like the product, don't buy it. I don't smoke but I don't condemn people who do."

However, Halloran's business has been good to him: in the past, on a good year, he'd purchase 1,000 to 1,500 pelts for manufacturing; this year, he bought 3,000, and next year he forecasts a need for 5,000. He attributes this entirely to an emerging demand for seal products in China:

> *"China has been a beacon of hope — they are just falling in love with seal products. I see this first hand every time I visit (I just returned last week). It is my mission to help save this industry and show it for what it truly is: the items we are producing now are amazing — fashion plus — and the Chinese are starting to see the same. It's about to explode; I know it and see it every visit."*

But China isn't the honeypot Halloran makes it out to be. While certain niche demands exist in Asia (seal penises are often purchased for fertility purposes, for instance), deals to distribute seal meat and oil on a larger scale have fallen through in recent years. Several Canadian politicians have declared that seal furs are "on their last legs," and that any gains retailers may be experiencing now will be short-lived.

Halloran's success is atypical in a market that for decades has been in a sharp decline.

A Dying Industry

Sealing was once a lucrative, burgeoning industry; today, it is on its way out.

Ten years ago, sealing was an industry with $34 million in annual sales; last year, that number was $1.5 million — $400,000 of which was overhead for sealers (boats, permits, guns, etc.). Though thousands of hunters are registered to hunt, only 390 actually participated, down from 6,000 a decade ago. In the past year, the number of sealing vessels has also decreased from 540 to 98.

With the implementation of the Seal Protection Regulations in 1965, the Canadian government established the first-ever set of limitations on the industry: set hunt dates, strict controls on killing methods, and the requirement of sealers and ship owners to be licensed. Six years later, in 1971, the first "kill quota" was set at 150,000 seals — an effort to monitor the industry. Over the years, the quota, or "total allowable catch," has gradually increased. By the end of the 1970s, it was set at 180,000; by 1990, it was 250,000; by the mid-2000s, it peaked at 350,000 seals.

To an outside observer, it would appear the industry has experienced growth and is demanding higher allowances, but this simply isn't true. While the quotas have increased, the "total catch" (actual number of seals killed) has dropped dramatically. In 2008, for example, 217,000 of 275,000 allowable seals were killed (79%); by 2013, only 17% of the quota was reached.

Canada's Department of Fisheries and Oceans cites an array of reasons for the decline in annual catch, from a strong Canadian dollar dampening export values to excessive ice cover, but the true source of the industry's decline can more likely be attributed to the decades-long anti-sealing battle staged by animal rights groups.

The Anti-Sealing Backlash

As early as the 1950s, animal rights groups surveyed Newfoundland seal fisheries and expressed concerns over the moral turpitude of the killing methods. But it wasn't until the mid-60s, when the northwest-Atlantic seal population declined by 50 percent, that activists launched into a full-fledged attack campaign.

Broadcast by the CBC in March of 1964, Les Phoques de la Banquise, or "The Great Seals of the Ice," chronicled the exploits of Canadian seal hunters; a scene showing a sealer skinning an animal alive and leaving it to wriggle on the ice sparked international outrage (the hunter later admitted he was paid by producers to commit the act, but the incident nevertheless catalyzed the anti-sealing movement). On the sole platform of "ending the commercial exploitation of seals," The International Fund for Animal Welfare (IFAW) established itself in 1969. The organization even hired Coca-Cola's advertising firm to launch a "Stop the Seal Hunt Campaign," which was wildly successful in boosting donations.

Protesters' efforts paid off. With the signing of 1972's Marine Mammal Protection Act, all seal products were banned in the United States (though it was a small market to begin with). In 1983, the European Union, responsible for importing 75% of Canadian seal pelts, implemented a permanent ban on "whitecoat" baby seal products. To add more misery for Canadian sealers, Safeway stores across Britain discontinued all Canadian fish products in protest. The ban tore apart the sealing community.

A major issue was the killing of "whitecoat" seals. From birth to two weeks old, harp seals have fluffy, white fur (this turns gray, brown, or spotted after two weeks). Traditionally, the majority of seals killed by hunters were baby whitecoats. Animal rights groups saw this practice as unsustainable and inhumane, and launched a campaign that would appeal to the masses: incredibly cute, big-eyed baby seals were juxtaposed with blood, guts, and murder. The Canadian government responded to the uproar by banning the hunting of whitecoats in 1987.

In recent years, continued efforts by the IFAW,

PETA, and The Humane Society have resulted in much more serious implications for sealers. Mexico banned all seal product imports in 2006; the European Union, which had previously banned only whitecoat imports, outlawed every seal import, regardless of age — a move that struck a permanent blow to the seal market. The Russian Federation, Taiwan, and others have since followed suit.

While the industry is nearly dead today, it still receives a tremendous amount of attention and coverage; PETA recently launched a celebrity seal campaign featuring the likes of Pamela Anderson and Perez Hilton, and lists the cause as its "top priority."

Inuits and Cultural Exemption

It is important to distinguish that most of the backlash against sealers is aimed at the commercialization of the trade; Inuits — the natives of Newfoundland who have subsisted on seals for hundreds of years — are nearly exempt from regulation. Though they only represent 3% of the seal trade, they have a separate hunt each year which is much less controlled.

For Inuit hunters, sealing isn't just a source of income — it's a way of life, and a keystone of their culture: the seal is their mainstay. Inuktitut vocabulary includes specific terms for "seal bone" and "seal fat," and legends are perpetuated within the culture of kinships and relationships with seals. In his 1991 study, *Animal Rights, Human Rights*, anthropologist George Wenzel spent two decades with Inuit sealers, and writes of "the impact of the animal rights movement upon the culture and economy of the Canadian Inuit." In his text, he argues that animal rights groups, while "well-meaning people," were full of misunderstanding and ignorance that "inflicted destruction on the vulnerable Inuit minority."

Due to such studies, Inuits have historically been given more leeway in international sealing bans (Europe included a clause in their 2006 seal product ban that allowed for Inuit natives to continue exporting in small numbers, for instance). But anti-sealing campaigns have purportedly had a negative impact on this community as well. Paul Irngaut, a wildlife communications advisor with Nunavut Tunngavik, speaks to the effects that a 1980s demonstration had on his village:

> *"In a small community like Resolute, income from sealing dropped from $54,000 in 1982 to $1,000 in 1983. Today, we still struggle. The income gained from seal hunts enables hunters to be able to feed and support their families, as well as other families...There once was a market for such goods, which would also support families and their ability to afford goods needed for hunting, and food to put on their table. Remember: Nunavut is a place where a cabbage can cost $28!"*

As Canada's National Inuit leader, Terry Audla represents 60,000 Inuits across the country. He says that the Inuit culture's traditional lifestyle requires the consumption of "free-roaming, nutrient-dense animals." Sealing, he argues, keeps his community alive. In a manifesto published online, Audla adds that "Inuits rely on the seal hunt for its shared market dynamics and the opportunity to sell seal pelts at fair market value," and that activists have "negatively impacted [sealers], along with other remote, coastal communities who have few other economic opportunities."

In April of 2014, talk show host Ellen Degeneres proclaimed her support for the Humane Society and its aim to end seal hunting; in response, Inuits took to Twitter to defend their "right." A sea of "Sealfies" emerged: Inuits and Canadian supporters alike posted photos of themselves clad in seal boots and jackets, and even sprawled half-naked across seal rugs. The campaign garnered national attention.

One 17-year-old Inuit, Killaq Enuaraq-Strauss, took to YouTube to express her disappointment with her favorite television personality:

> *"You're an inspiration as a woman but*
> *also as a human being, but let me educate*
> *you a bit on seal hunting in the Canadian*
> *arctic. We do not hunt seals ... for fashion.*
> *We hunt to survive. I own sealskin boots*
> *and they are super cute, and I am proud to*
> *say that I own them, and I also eat seal*
> *meat more times than I can count. But I*
> *can't apologize for that."*

The Humane Society was quick to clarify that it didn't oppose the Inuit hunt — only the commercial hunt; PETA operates with the same ideology. The organization's spokeswoman, Danielle Katz, says her organization is primarily interested in the commercial hunt, which accounts for "97% of the seals that are killed," and says the "Inuit sealers are under no threat" in the seal market.

In the grand scheme of the industry, sealing isn't lucrative for anyone: sealers struggle to get by, the government wastes time and resources on a dying trade, and groups like PETA and the Humane Society have spent millions combatting one of the world's smallest commercial fur markets.

The Cute Bias

While those involved in the seal trade maintain that it's humane, sustainable, and well-regulated, animal rights activists and protesters call the practice cold-blooded and barbaric. One question lingers: why so much undying support for protecting seals in particular?

There is a compelling case to be made that sealing is particularly demonized due to the fact that the animals are cute and fuzzy, a fact animal rights groups have consistently relied on for campaigns. The imagery used by PETA, The Humane Society, and other activist groups is striking and consistent: big mammalian eyes, fuzzy snow-colored fur, blood against white ice — cuteness (juxtaposed with violence) has been employed to garner public interest, and it has worked.

Harp Seals, an activist group working to end the Canadian seal slaughter, conjures such language to mobilize people to join their cause. Seal pups are "famous for their big black eyes and fluffy white fur," they write, "and are astounding in their innocence, individuality, gentle nature, and beauty." The language appeals to society's predisposition for pedomorphism, or things that resemble human babies (big eyes, fuzzy little heads, etc.); social psychologists have long argued that these traits are what make cute creatures endearing.

Regardless of cuteness, the harp seal population in Canada is currently estimated at 5.6 million — nearly triple what it was in the 1970s — and with nearly 20,000 species threatened by extinction, the populous animal seems a strange target for so much attention. Renowned ecologist Jacques Cousteau addresses this:

> *"The harp seal question is entirely*
> *emotional. We have to be logical. We have*
> *to aim our activity first to the endangered*
> *species. Those who are moved by the plight*

of the harp seal could also be moved by the
plight of the pig...We have to be logical. If
we are sentimental about harp seals,
which are not endangered because they
are partially protected, then we have to
also be emotional about pigs."

Dr. M. Sanjayan, a noted conservationist, believes that non-profits and animal protection agencies have a deeply flawed selection methodology rooted almost solely in "preserving cute and fuzzy animals" rather than the creatures that "actually keep our planet humming." He touches on this in an interview with *National Geographic*:

"What we decide to save really is very
arbitrary—it's much more often done for
emotional or psychological or national
reasons than would ever be made with a
model...people end up saving what they
want to save—it's as simple as that."

Sanjayan cites ants as a prime example of how activists are biased toward cuteness over ecological function. The tiny creatures are essential environmental helpers — they disseminate seeds, aerate soils, and eliminate human pests — but are not represented by animal rights groups. "If we're going to save pandas, for instance, rather than ants," adds Marc Bekoff, an ethologist at the University of Colorado Boulder, "we need a good reason, and being cute is not a good reason."

In Western society, cows are on the opposite spectrum of the cute bias. Every year in the United States, 40 million cattle are slaughtered; their skin, manufactured into leather, accounts for 50% of their total byproduct value. We're the world's largest producer of hides, with an annual supply of 1.1 million tons. Most commercial cattle endure horrendous living conditions: they're crowded into factory farms with inadequate food and water, pumped full of antibiotics, and spend their entire lives milling around on concrete floors without the "luxury" of living in their natural habitats.

Cows are killed by a swift blow to the skull with a stun gun, and a slit to the throat; they are then hooked to a chain by their hind leg, and bled out over a tub — often still alive, but not coherent. Under the U.S.'s 1958 Humane Slaughter Act, this is not only legal, but considered a "compassionate" way to die. Chickens endure even worse: they are hung upside down, shocked into paralysis, then drowned in hot water. The act of seal clubbing, when gauged with these methods, seems somewhat tamer, but has been sensationalized as unapologetically violent due to the fact that seals are more aesthetically pleasing than cows and chickens.

Whales present a case that isn't entirely dissimilar. Beneath hotly-contested Canadian ice, the giant, unattractive creatures go unloved. Recently, the Canadian government moved to take humpback whales off the threatened species list; instead, the animals will be labeled a "species of special concern" — a title that comes with limited protective privileges. According to *Reuters*, the change of classification means "the humpback's habitat would no longer be protected under Canada's Species at Risk Act, thereby removing some of the risk of legal battles with environmental groups."

Yet above ice, seals continue to be a success story. They've been haloed by legislation, defended by celebrities, and largely protected from the force of whooshing clubs. It seems that, at least in this case, cuteness ensures conservation.

3.

WHY IS ART EXPENSIVE?

In 1996, an art dealer named Glafira Rosales approached Ann Freedman, the president of New York's Knoedler Gallery, which sold artwork to wealthy collectors for over 150 years. Rosales offered to sell Knoedler paintings by masters like Mark Rothko, Jackson Pollock and Willem de Kooning at bargain prices — under one million dollars each.

She told Freedman that an anonymous collector — a family friend — inherited the paintings and recently rediscovered them. For over a decade, the gallery resold the pieces for millions and stored its files on the acquired works under the label "Secret Santa." Pushed for more details about the mysterious collector, Rosales replied, "Don't kill the goose that's laying the golden egg."

Fifteen years after Roales first approached Knoedler, a Belgian hedge fund manager named Pierre Lagrange received bad news. A consultant that he hired to investigate the authenticity of a $17 million Jackson Pollock painting he bought from the gallery discovered a pigment of paint that was not sold commercially during Pollock's lifetime. When Lagrange emailed Knoedler, the gallery closed. Within a year, several other customers joined him in claiming that their multimillion dollar purchases were "worthless fakes." In 2013, Rosales pled guilty in a $80 million forgery case.

The case of these forged masterworks highlights just how difficult it is to pin down the source of art's financial value. Until Lagrange complained, the paintings were worth millions, praised as masterpieces, and exhibited to appreciative audiences. The revelation of the real artist as Pei-Shen Qian, a 73 year-old Chinese immigrant who painted the forgeries from his garage in Queens for a few thousand dollars each, rendered them instantly worthless. Yet the paintings' appearance did not change. An artwork's aesthetics, the feelings it conveys, and anything else that derives from its physical appearance may influence its price, but as Qian's paintings demonstrate, they cannot explain its extraordinary value.

This points to an important if unromantic truth: brands are king in fine art; names like Rothko and Pollock distinguish them from unknown artists as Coke and Pepsi do from other sugar water. Qian painted attractive works in the style of famous artists, yet attaching the names Rothko and Pollock increased the paintings' value by millions of dollars.

One reason wealthy individuals spend millions collecting fine art is that brands like Picasso and Monet have staying power. Buying a million dollar painting at Sotheby's is not like buying a Lamborghini. A car's value falls as soon as it is driven off the lot; a Picasso painting retains its value and even appreciates over time. But amidst the uncertainty of subjective taste, how does an artist establish herself as a million dollar brand? How can a Manhattan socialite buy a $100,000 abstract painting by an emerging artist without fearing that it will be a tacky, $250 wall decoration in a few years? In other words, how does some paint splashed on a canvas become expensive, and how does it stay expensive over time?

The answer is that the market for fine art is heavily "curated." It is controlled by galleries and dealers who commit with astonishing discipline to keeping artwork prices predictable and pegged to signals of quality like the prestigiousness of the gallery selling the artist's work. You could say the market for art is "rigged"; a more charitable explanation is that galleries and dealers act as tastemakers, deciding which art is good and therefore expensive. The end result is to turn artists into brands, which introduces enough certainty for the market to function.

The Artist as an Asset Class

During record breaking art auctions at Christie's and Sotheby's, the amount of money spent often exceeds the gross domestic product of small island nations. As an outsider, it's hard to see results like Christie's $745 million contemporary art auction in May of 2013 as anything other than a pissing contest of conspicuous consumption. Yet insiders in the art market describe these purchases as investments.

If anyone has reason to be skeptical of the enormous sums paid for fine art, Filippo Guerrini-Maraldi ranks among them. As the Executive Director and Head of the Fine Art Team at R.K. Harrison Insurance Services, Guerrini-Maraldi insures art collections worth millions of dollars, a sum for which R.K. Harrison's insurance brokers are liable. Yet the team never declines to insure, say, a pleasant painting of four rectangles at a six figure price tag. "If I am asked to insure a work of art that someone bought from a dealer or auction house," Guerrini-Maraldi tells us, "who am I to say, 'You paid too much mate?'"

R.K. Harrison can usually insure works for the value the client cites because fine art has held its value over time. While conceding that there are "heavily inflated prices for works of art" as certain artists or periods come in vogue, Guerrini-Maraldi notes that "there are corrections, just like with stock market bubbles." This stability has been endorsed by the financial sector, which accepts art collections as collateral.

"The idea that art is an asset class and that certain objects by certain artists retain their value," says Jonathan Binstock, who has a doctorate in art history and helps clients assemble art collections as part of Citi Private Bank's Art Advisory service, "is something people around the world have come to agree upon." As William Fleischer, owner of Bernard Fleischer & Sons, an art insurance broker, points out, it's really no different than the high prices people pay for collectibles ranging from comic books to antique toothpick holders.

The consensus on fine art's value is also a data-driven conclusion. Binstock notes that between art databases of auction sale results that date back to the eighties, and published volumes that go back even further, there is "a lot of history to justify the price one might have to pay" for a highly-priced artwork. Any number of favorable analyses chart the prices of pieces by renowned artists like Andy Warhol. Despite a rapid rise and fall in price during exuberant periods like the 2008 fine art bubble, they outperform the stock market over several decades.

So how do you evaluate an artwork's worth? According to Sara Friedlander, who organizes art auctions at Christie's, the world's largest auction house, "There is not one art market. Every artist has his or her own market." Christie's predicts auction prices by looking at "comparables in the market," which except in the case of real outliers or a rare masterpiece, means the selling price of a similar work by the same artist.

In one sense, this demonstrates how artwork maintains its diversity despite its commodification; there is a near infinite supply of art out there, but a limited supply of Van Goghs. In another sense, this gets at how the overwhelming factor underlying the price of an artwork is the artists' brand. The art world refers to buying "a Pollock" or "a Warhol" because those artists are brands, and the contemporary art market is more like the music scene of 50 years ago, which celebrated the full albums of a select few bands, than the music scene today, which more often celebrates a few singles by a wider array of bands.

Critics are less sanguine about investing in Warhols, Rothkos, and Richters. In The Supermodel and the Brillo Box, economist Don Thompson writes that positive headlines about the sums fetched at auction by fine art ignore when those works sold at a higher price years earlier. As the Financial Times notes, Thompson's book fits into a string of recent commentary that "points out the huge pitfalls of buying art for investment: sky-high levels of risk, illiquidity, and a fashion-driven nature that can see last year's 'in' artists fail even to be accepted for resale by the big auction houses."

That doesn't necessarily mean the perception of fine art as an investment is a mirage. The possibility that the work of a young artist will shoot up in price from $10,000 to $100,000 appeals to speculators and entails risk. A Gerhard Richter piece is like a blue chip stock; a work by a fashionable young artist is more like funding a startup. Many startups fail; some blue chip stocks turn out to be Enron. Picking individual stocks has always been a risky, high variance strategy rather than prudent investing. Yet that has not kept wealthy investors away.

William Fleischer says that some collectors he insures "store art in warehouses, purely for the investment." Flipping art happens; the fastest growing product at Artnet, which publishes market research on fine art, is its online auctions that "offer quick transactions at low costs." But especially at the top of the market, financial returns are a secondary concern.

Jonathan Binstock advises some of the world's top collectors from his post at Citi Private Bank, yet neither he nor any of his colleagues are bankers. He describes their role as helping clients assemble collections that are "culturally significant and more valuable than the sum total of prices paid." Personal preferences matter as much or more than return on investment. Their clients don't "buy a painting for $5 million because we think it will be worth 2% more in 3 years," he says. "And they rarely sell."

Art is not the most sound investment, but it pays incredible dividends in the form of social cachet. As Don Thompson notes, every newspaper covered Leon Black's purchase of Edvard Munch's "The Scream" for $120 million; buying a "moderately impressive yacht" for the same amount garners almost no publicity at all. Top collectors enjoy preferential access to famous artwork, and seating charts at art fairs and auctions carefully reflect a collector's status. Collectors buy an experience and standing as much as an expensive product; Jackson Pollock paintings essentially serve as the admission ticket to one of the world's wealthiest and most exclusive clubs. Christie's estimates the market for artwork priced over $20 million at roughly 150 collectors.

According to Sara Friedlander of Christie's, "since the earliest days of the Renaissance, art has been a way to enter into certain social circles. That's a good thing." Whether spending $10,000 or $50 million, she says, collectors can interact with artists and support the arts like Renaissance Italy's Medici family. More cynically, lending Picassos to exhibits and donating millions to museums allows heirs, hedge fund traders, and Fortune 500 executives to enjoy coverage as cultured patrons of the arts.

A final reason people buy heinously expensive art? "After you have a fourth home and a G5 jet," one wealthy collector told Sarah Thornton, author of Seven Days In The Art World, "what else is there?"

Are Masterpieces Special?

If you ask anyone in the world to name a famous painting, by far the most common response will be the Mona Lisa. Art historians have offered many explanations for its signature status; the Louvre website cites, among others, the subject's enigmatic smile and novel features like its three-quarters pose. But in an article for Intelligent Life, journalist Ian Leslie suggests an alternative explanation: that the Mona Lisa's ascension to the top of the art world, like that of any artwork, was a historical accident.

Despite its fame, the Mona Lisa has a surprisingly sleepy history. "In the 1850s, Leonardo da Vinci was considered no match for giants of Renaissance art like Titian and Raphael," Leslie writes, "whose works were worth almost ten times as much as the 'Mona Lisa.'" The Mona Lisa hung in the Louvre, but it did not attract crowds. That changed in 1911, when a museum employee hid in a closet overnight and walked out the next day with the Mona Lisa hidden under an artist's frock. Suddenly the Mona Lisa was front page news around the world. When the thief was arrested, it fed a media spectacle around his trial, as the Italian native defended his theft as a patriotic act.

Within psychology departments, it is established that familiarity breeds likeability. Psychologist James Cutting sees this "mere-exposure effect" as explaining why we celebrate some paintings over others. In an experiment, he showed undergraduates a slideshow of Impressionist paintings. A control group liked the paintings that filled art history textbooks; students shown comparable yet unheralded works four times as often as the famous paintings preferred the lesser known paintings. Following this logic, we can see how coverage of the Mona Lisa theft made its reputation and how each masterpiece may owe its status to historical accidents. Leslie writes:

> *"The most reproduced works of impressionism today tend to have been bought by five or six wealthy and influential collectors in the late 19th century. The preferences of these men bestowed prestige on certain works, which made the works more likely to be hung in galleries and printed in anthologies. The kudos cascaded down the years, gaining momentum from mere exposure as it did so. The more people were exposed to, say, 'Bal du Moulin de la Galette,' the more they liked it, and the more they liked it, the more it appeared in books, on posters and in big exhibitions. Meanwhile, academics and critics created sophisticated justifications for its pre-eminence."*

Other circumstances external to an artwork also impact its status in the art world. One reason we celebrate certain works and artists is their contribution to artistic movements. "The Fountain" is just a urinal placed upside down and signed, but it defined the Dada movement's challenge to artistic sensibilities, which is why an authorized copy of the artwork (the original was lost) sold for $1.8 million in 1999. Yet this meaning is an ever-changing judgment. According to Jonathan Binstock of Citi Private Bank, Piero della Francesca, an early Renaissance painter, was "out of favor for a long time." When surrealists like Salvador Dali began to use his artwork as inspiration, however, museums recognized him as a precedent for an influential art movement. "Now he's everybody's favorite," say Binstock. When we say artwork has value, really we value the social meaning we ascribe to it: transient characteristics like its current meaning within the artistic canon, contemporary attitudes about art, and the favorability built up over time by its ubiquity.

While this casts some doubt on our celebration of select masterpieces, it does not mean that artistic intentions and craftsmanship play no role. In his article, Leslie points to another experiment that mimicked Cutter's setup, but included work by painter Thomas Kinkade, whose fairy tale-perfect landscapes are often cited as bad, kitschy art. Just as any number of good movies can endear themselves over many viewings, but watching a bad movie will only make you hate it more, the students disliked Kinkade the more they saw his work.

The beneficiaries of these historical accidents — the Mona Lisas and the Guernicas, the da Vincis and the Picassos — are highly valued. Yet the artists that monopolize record setting auctions represent a tiny portion of the market — around forty artists, according to Jonathan Binstock. Collectors confidently shell out for artists who dominate art history textbooks. But what about young artists? Or deceased artists who the art world is still deciding whether to celebrate as an influential master or leave as a footnote? How exactly does canvas and paint get anointed as expensive art?

The First Rule of Art Collection

When Daniel Radcliffe, who has established himself as a contemporary art collector with the riches he earned from portraying Harry Potter in film, attended the Frieze Art Fair, he set his sights on a work by conceptual artist Jim Hodges. The wealthy actor was good for the money, but he discovered that an ability to pay does not easily translate to the ability to buy an artwork. The dealer told Radcliffe that he was "waiting for a more prestigious collector" to buy the work; Radcliffe only managed to buy the painting after the artist personally lobbied the dealer.

When you ask industry insiders about fine art prices, they attribute them to supply and demand. "It's a market like any other," we heard again and again. Yet that is not exactly accurate. When shopping for luxury goods, customers often equate price with quality. This is particularly true in the fine art market, where the diversity of offerings and vagaries of taste make consensus about value impossible to achieve without the signaling quality of brands. No one considers a painting selling for lower than expected a fortuitous discount; they perceive it as a sign that the artist was overhyped and overpriced.

As a result, art galleries exercise a level of control over prices that, as economist Allison Schrager writes in Quartz, "would be illegal in most industries." In this way, artists' work gets singled out and begins to enjoy the compounding benefits of the mere exposure effect. It's not exactly a "historical accident," as Leslie describes it, but part of a carefully orchestrated process that turns artists into established brands.

The majority of new artwork is sold at galleries, and artists often sell their artwork through a single gallery, which represents the artist and typically takes a 50% commission on each sale. Galleries use their position as the pipeline of new artwork to establish a certain level of price stability in the fine art market, without which it would be too risky for millionaires to drop big money on anything but fully established artists like Rothko.

The first way galleries do this is by refusing to drop the price of any artwork. Galleries have their own reputation for dealing work at a certain price point; to protect the prestige of the gallery and their artists, they will drop an artist whose work fails to sell rather than reduce the price. So within the gallery at least, the price of a painting never drops, instead the artist just fades away.

But galleries are equally worried about a piece by one of their artists quickly reselling at a high price (especially it they won't receive a commission for the sale), since any downward trend in price tarnishes an artist's brand. So gallerists maintain control over prices by dealing with trusted clients who will only sell through the gallery and at its prices. They do this through the use of both carrots (galleries offer loyal collectors preferred access to their best offerings) and sticks (galleries may stop selling to collectors who resell their inventory on the secondary market). Allison Schrager offers the following anecdote about a collector offered enough money for a painting by a celebrity that "she'd never have to work again":

> *"She explained that she would not bargain with [the celebrity] — any resale of the painting must go through the gallery, so [the gallery would] get a commission and select the price—not her. The young collector knew there would be consequences to making the sale. She may have owned the painting, but reselling it at a profit without the gallery's permission would blackball her from the art industry. To her, that was not worth the millions she was offered."*

Galleries do, of course, want their artists to succeed and the price of their artwork to increase. They just need to make sure it happens in lockstep with validating critical reception. So in addition to introducing artists to the right people and getting them studio time, galleries make an exception to the practice of never dropping an artist's price for particularly influential collectors or museums, who receive preferred access to artwork, since that boosts an artist's standing.

Auction houses threaten galleries' control over prices and commissions. One employee at an auction house who chose to remain anonymous conceded that tension exists between galleries and auction houses. Although he believes auctions play an important role in driving up the price point for artists' work, gallerists dislike seeing art prices at the whims of the market. When artwork does hit the secondary market, galleries attend the auction and, if necessary, bid on their artist's work to make sure its price does not fall. "I call it support bidding," Guerrini-Maraldi tells us. "It happens a lot when people want to protect their portfolio or interest in the artist." (Like a gallery with a vested interest, someone who has many Rothkos, for example, may bid up the price to maintain the value of her own collection.)

Although auction houses submit artwork to the forces of supply and demand, they also intervene to ensure that the market is gentle. To reassure sellers, Christie's and Sotheby's commonly guarantee that they will not sell a work below a minimum "reserve price." Sensitive to the brand damage caused by a painting failing to sell, when no one bids above the reserve price, auctioneers may pretend to spot a high bid in the back, slam their hammer down, and yell "Sold!". Another common tactic is to "bid off the chandelier" by calling out a few nonexistent bids to start the bidding. Auction houses also may prime a market by showcasing works of an artist up for sale at exhibits around the world — seemingly grasping the power of mere exposure. Even more deceptively, as the New York Times notes, "collectors can find themselves being bid up by someone who, in exchange for agreeing in advance to pay a set amount for a work, is promised a cut of anything that exceeds that price," which inflates prices through false competition.

"The art market is the largest unregulated market in the world," Filippo Guerrini-Maraldi reflects during our conversation, echoing a common refrain on the world of posh galleries and auction houses. "There are very few rules. People can behave in extraordinary ways."

Curating Status Symbols

Investigating the fine art market makes it clear that millionaires' conspicuous consumption strongly influences which art gets elevated and celebrated over others. In the art market's defense, the Renaissance model of a few rich families acting as artistic patrons is often praised. Galleries characterize their actions as in the best interest of the artists, and the anonymous auction employee we spoke to praised gallerists' role as "real visionaries who select this roster where we can really feel that this artist is in the same program as the estate of Pablo Picasso." Sure, galleries are brand managers, but they can also be seen as the equivalent of museum curators.

At the same time, he admires the more democratic aspect of public purchases on the secondary market, where artwork can speak for itself. Ultimately, price manipulation semi-arbitrarily turns a select few artists into lucrative brands and status symbols. As one art dealer admits, "sometimes you can get an equally attractive work on the street, for a fraction of the price, but you miss the investment value and social prestige of building a collection."

Yet it's also important to remember that while galleries and auction houses control the money spigot,
they don't exercise sole control over critical taste. Citi
Private Bank's Jonathan Binstock describes the relationship between the market and museums as a two
way street. He notes that "there are younger artists who
gain a lot of traction in the market and, at least in part
for this reason, museums begin to take notice and give
them extra consideration." Binstock also mentions
artists whose prices inflated during a craze for a certain
style in the 1980s, then returned to earth once the
market moved on. And alternatives to the gallery model
— like selling directly to customers online or through
nonprofit spaces — allow artists to fund their work
without adhering to the tastes and controls of
traditional galleries.

Money does influence art. Paintings that look good
on the walls of Manhattan apartments sell more easily,
and in a complete violation of supply and demand,
since exposure and evidence of successful sales boost
prices, the market rewards prolificness over spending
years on a few masterpieces. But no amount of intervention can indefinitely prop up the price of a work
that museum curators shun; Emma Webster, a young
artist with whom we discussed the financial side of art
after a showing in San Francisco, tells us, "It's impossible to make art for the market. Artists that try to cling
to fads are easy to find and disregard."

Still, the fine art market plays a large role in defining
which art is important. And as a result, so too do the
heirs and hedge fund managers that supply the money.
As the Mona Lisa anecdote suggests, which artwork get
singled out as masterpieces may always be partly arbitrary. But even the artists whose work sells for hundreds of thousands or millions of dollars might prefer
that branding — and the snobbery and cult of personality that is the byproduct of marketing artists' work as

worth a fortune — play less of a role in deciding which pieces are celebrated. "Famous artists do not create the aura," Webster says. "It is the gallery, promoter, critic, and buyer, all of whom are more willing to uphold these pillars of pretension so that their investments can maintain power."

The galleries and auction houses of the fine art market loom large in the art world. By connecting artists, curators, and collectors, they support and celebrate artists. But it is their ability to turn unknown artists into famous brands and disparate artwork into stable investments that has truly achieved an art form.

4.

HOW TO CHARGE $1,000 FOR ABSOLUTELY NOTHING

In early 2008, developer Armin Heinrich sat down at his desk to design an app for the newly released iPhone. It had to be a moneymaker, he figured; more importantly, it had to demonstrate his sense of humor. Ultimately, he settled on an idea that kept his input costs extremely low and his potential profits high: he'd develop an app that did absolutely nothing, for which the buyer would pay an absurdly high price — the highest in the entire app store.

His app, "I Am Rich" did just that: for $999.99 (the steepest price for an app that Apple allows), a purchaser would gain access to the app — nothing more than a glowing, red orb. But having the ruby on your screen meant that you were rich — clearly you had to be, to afford to pay $1,000 for something utterly useless. Heinrich's intention was to create the ultimate Veblen good in app form: something desirable merely due to it's price and exclusivity. With an enticing description, "I Am Rich" was listed in Apple's app store on August 5, 2008:

"The red icon on your iPhone or iPod touch always reminds you (and others when you show it to them) that you were able to afford this.

It's a work of art with no hidden function at all.

After pressing the (i) on the main page, a secret mantra will be shown. This may help you to stay rich, healthy and successful."

Shockingly, in a span of just a few hours, 8 people purchased the app — 5 in the United States, one in Germany, and one in France. But Heinrich's original plan had failed: it wasn't being bought by rich folks looking to show it off, but rather by curious people who thought it was a joke. One reviewer (Lee5279xx) was so riled up that he was actually charged for the application he'd just purchased, that he wrote a ranting review:

"This is not a joke! I need someone from apple to help me with this scam. I saw this app with a few friends and we jokingly clicked 'buy' thinking it was a JOKE, to see what would happen....I called my visa card and they verified I was charged $999.99. THIS IS NO JOKE. DO NOT BUY THIS APP. BEWARE..."

Less than a full day after hitting the app store, Apple removed it with no explanation — but not before Heinrich had made away with $5,600 (after Apple had taken it's 30% "store upkeep fee" of $2,400). "I have no idea why they [took it down]," he told the Los Angeles

Times in an interview a few days later, "and I'm not aware of any violation of the rules to sell software on the app store." Heinrich hadn't, in fact, broken any of Apple's guidelines, but the company, to this day, has never addressed its propensity for selectively taking down apps it deems unfit.

In the aftermath of the "I Am Rich" debacle, two of the eight buyers extensively complained to Apple and were given full refunds. "I don't want to collect money from people who did this by accident," Heinrich later said. "I am glad that Apple returned the money for two orders." But Heinrich also admitted that he was a bit disappointed about his creation's short lifespan, as he felt there was a demand for it. "I am sure a lot more people would like to buy it — but currently can't do so. The app is a work of art and included a 'secret mantra' — that's all." Multiple customers, he adds, emailed him saying they loved the app and had "no trouble spending the money" (though this was never verified).

And what exactly was the secret mantra that his customers had supposedly "raved" about having access to? Let's just say that it must've taken a special buyer to see a thousand dollars of value in it (notice the artistic lack of punctuation and the fashionable misspelling of "deserve"):

I AM RICH
I DESERV IT
I AM GOOD, HEALTHY &
SUCCESSFUL

The following year, due to popular demand, Heinrich, released "I Am Rich LE," a more affordable version priced at $9.99; it's still available for purchase today. This time around, the app even houses a few features (due to Apple's policy that an app must contain some sort of "definable content"): a calculator for "basic financial calculations," an ""in-built help system," and the "famous mantra — without the spelling mistakes."

To date, the app has 70 reviews, and holds an average 2.5 star (out of 5) rating — though most of the one-star ratings are due to the fact that the app actually contains something useful. "Can you please make this app so it does absolutely nothing like the first one?" implores one customer. "I didn't buy this app to get my money's worth."

"It's art and it's brilliant," writes another, more satisfied buyer. "Not everything you pay for has to have value. Screw practicality."

5.

IS WINE BULLSHIT?

Many oenophiles consider Château Lafite Rothschild Bordeaux the world's greatest wine. In the 17th century, both the British prime minister and King Louis XV drank it regularly. In 1855, when Napoleon instructed French wine experts to classify France's Bordeaux wines, Lafite Rothschild earned a top spot as a Premier Cru, a rank it maintains to this day.

Thomas Jefferson ranked among its admirers. In 1985, a 1787 bottle of Lafite Bordeaux that Jefferson supposedly owned sold at auction for a record $156,000. Chateau Lafite Rothschild released their most recent Bordeaux for 420 euros a bottle. Older bottles command prices higher than $1,000.

Wine experts discuss Lafite as if tasting an ever-changing Impressionist painting. "The wine still has a dark ruby/purple color and an extraordinarily youthful nose of graphite, black currants, sweet, unsmoked cigar tobacco, and flowers," influential American wine critic Robert Parker wrote on the 2000 Lafite. "I originally predicted that it would first reach maturity in 2011, but I would push that back by 5-7 years now."

The most highly imported wine in America, in contrast, is Yellow Tail. An Australian wine known best for its colorful labels featuring a kangaroo, it sells for around $7 a bottle. The winery produces 12 million cases a year, and one theory for its successful conquest of the American wine market in the early 2000s is that it created a simple, sweet wine that appealed to the 85% of Americans who don't really like wine. With price tags that differ by several orders of magnitude, Lafite Bordeaux and budget wines like Yellow Tail inhabit different worlds.

Despite these differences, it's unclear whether anyone can tell the difference between a $2,000 Lafite Bordeaux and a $3 table wine. In fact, many wine economists consider the matter settled. Blind tastings and academic studies robustly show that neither amateur consumers nor expert judges can consistently differentiate between fine wines and cheap wines, nor identify the flavors within them. But if a $10, $100, and $1,000 bottle of wine all taste roughly the same in a blind taste test, how do you explain their different price tags?

How We Produce 23 Billion Liters of Wine

Wine is simply fermented grape juice, but its production is a finicky process. Differences in the production of bottom and top-shelf wines parallel the gap between how Burger King and an upscale restaurant make their burgers.

Asked about the keys to winemaking, the proprietor of Domaine Dujac, which makes an expensive French Burgundy, responded, "The soil, the soil, and the soil." In fertile soil, grapes fill with water that dilutes the flavor. Only grapes grown on rocky, challenging land stay flavorful. Characteristics of the soil also impact taste, as do the climate and topography. The French use the term "terroir" to express how these characteristics flavor wine.

Lafite treats viniculture as art. Its soil of gravel, sand, and limestone in the Medoc region of France results in low yields but flavorful grapes. The winery tries various combinations of grapes in pursuit of the best possible vintage. Only grapes grown in its best soil are bottled as premier cru (first growth) Bordeaux. The rest are bottled as a "second growth" that sells for a fraction of the price. Total production is under 100,000 cases a year, on-site coopers make wooden barrels specially suited to imparting flavor, and staff light candles in the tasting area before wine is sampled. Although not every wine benefits from extensive aging, Lafite Bordeaux ages for a decade or more before maturing into complex flavors.

Charles Shaw wine — nicknamed "Two-Buck Chuck" because it first sold at Trader Joe's supermarkets for $1.99 — inhabits the other pole of the wine market. The makers, the Bronco Wine Company, grow grapes in California's Central Valley. The soil is considered too fertile to produce flavorful grapes, but produces high yields.

The process is an economy of scale par excellence. Once picked, grapes are processed and bottled in "a high-speed bottling plant capable of churning out 18 million cases of wine a year, double the annual production of all the rest of Napa Valley." Bronco also buys surplus wine from other California vineyards at bargain prices.

Owner Frank Franzia doesn't bother with notions of terroir. All the wine is blended together, regardless of its origin. In 2003, Bronco processed 300,000 tons of grapes to make 20 million cases of wine, of which a quarter are Charles Shaw wines. Asked how he sells wine for the same price as a bottle of water, Franzia responded, "They're overcharging for the water. Don't you get it?"

Wineries fall in a continuum between the artisanal and industrial poles represented by these two wineries. But there is not a neat correlation between size and industrial practices, on one hand, and price and perceived prestige on the other. A tiny winery that refuses to use artificial fertilizers and pesticides may sell its wine for $10-$20.

Nor does every bottle of wine sell under the label of the winery where its grapes were grown. Every year, wineries make more wine than they can sell. Wineries produced 26.38 billion liters of wine in 2010, but the world consumed only 23.21 billion liters. Wine merchants called negociants buy some of this surplus to sell under their own name and label. Cameron Hughes, an American negociant, sells roughly 400,000 cases of wine a year at prices ranging from $10 to $60 a bottle. In addition, giant labels like Charles Shaw and Yellow Tail, despite having their own vineyards, mostly buy and blend other wineries' grapes. For some wineries, selling to negociants or the Bronco Wine Company is a shameful necessity. Other wineries, especially smaller ones focused on the winemaking process, are happy to have someone do the sales work.

Just four countries, Italy, France, the United States, and Spain, produce 58% of the world's wine; they also consume 40% of it. The market for fine wines, however, is more globalized; Chateau Lafite Rothschild exported 75% of its premier cru in 2008.

Pricing Wine

While the Bronco Wine Company and Lafite Rothschild produce wine in very different ways, that disparity alone cannot explain the huge variation in wine prices. But it is helpful. According to Troy Carter, founder of Motorcycle Wineries in San Francisco, wine consists of two distinct markets: one is industrial, efficient, and cheap; the other is romantic and expensive.

Cheap, industrial wine constitutes the majority of what the world drinks. Among Americans who drink wine regularly, only 12% spend $30 or more on a bottle each month. The U.S. imports more Yellow Tail — the budget Australian wine — each year than the total number of bottles imported from France. Carter estimates that 90% of wine by volume is under $10 a bottle, and he says that in this part of the market, production and distribution costs determine prices.

Troy Carter describes the distribution process for a wine that sells for about $30 — the process that applies to the cheap wine market and much of the romantic wine industry — as follows. Wine is widely dispersed to stores, supermarkets, restaurants, and private collectors by wine merchants and distributors, as wineries avoid these responsibilities. Distributors buy cases of wine from the maker at $15 per bottle. They then sell it to restaurants and stores for $20.

Restaurants' markups vary, but stores consistently sell it for $29. Vacationers in Napa Valley will pay $30 to buy the bottle directly from the winery. It is something of a standard that bottles cost one dollar less at stores than at wineries. Supermarket chains like Costco, which is the largest provider of wine in the U.S., sell the bottle for around $22 — just above wholesale prices.

For cheaper wines, the economics of distribution work similarly. When you buy a $7 bottle of Yellow Tail chardonnay, that somehow covers the production cost, taxes, import duties, and various markups.

The boundaries are fuzzy, but as you look at the pricing of mid-range wines that cost from $10 to $70, the rules are less and less straightforward. That wholesale price, and the price consumers ultimately pay, become disentangled from marginal production costs. At $50, Carter tells us, pricing is nearly independent of production costs.

In this range, brands can dramatically affect price. The same wine in two differently branded bottles can have very different costs, as shown by the prices offered by negociants such as Cameron Hughes. In the Washington Post, wine columnist Dave McIntyre observes:

> *"Hughes signs confidentiality agreements that preserve a winery's anonymity. After all, a producer of a $40 Napa Valley cabernet sauvignon doesn't want his customers to know they can get a nearly identical wine from Hughes for $25. Yet the winery might need to move out surplus inventory, generate cash flow or make full use of capacity, a win-win-win situation for the producers, consumers and Hughes."*

The region of origin also significantly impacts price. Wines from Napa, for example, are 61% more expensive than other Californian wines. This partly reflects differences in quality, as Napa's soil and many of its winemakers are well regarded. It also speaks to the branding power of certain regions. There is a reason that Napa winemakers cry foul when Frank Franzia labels Charles Shaw as Napa wine (his offices are in Napa), even though the grapes come from the Central Valley.

Reviews by prominent wine critics can also send the price of a wine soaring. As an Atlantic article said of Robert Parker, the world's most influential wine critic who reviews fine wine but also wines as inexpensive as $20:

> *"A positive review and a score over 90, especially for a wine that is produced in*

*small quantities, can ignite speculation
that sends the price rocketing and clears
the wine out of the stores."*

A mix of production and distribution costs, brand reputation, pricing strategies, and quality and critical reception determine prices of mid-range wines. There are some pricing anomalies, but for the most part, the market for wines in the $4 to $70 range operate like a typical consumer market. When Yellow Tail's kangaroo logo helped it dominate the U.S. wine market, it led to an avalanche of wines labelled with colorful critters. That may clash with the refined image of wine, but it's the type of standard beverage industry fare that actually governs the majority of wine sold by volume.

Fine wines, however, are a different beast. Almost entirely cachet, their prices rise and fall with little connection to quality.

Speculating In Human Snobbery

One night, this author found himself at a dinner party at a billionaire's house. After the meal, the host gave a tour of his wine cellar. "The best part of having a wine cellar," he confided, "is that you can drink thousands of dollars of wine for free."

He accomplished this by taking advantage of how wines' price and quality increase as they age. Until the turn of the millenium, oenophiles wealthy enough to sit on thousand dollar cases of wine dabbled in wine "investing," usually with a glass of Bordeaux in hand. As Darius Sanai described it in GQ:

> *"For centuries, investing in wine was
> fairly straight forward. You would buy as
> many cases of classed-growth claret en
> primeur (as futures) as your budget*

*allowed, watch their value double over the
next few years, take delivery of half of
them, and sell the remainder to recoup
your initial investment. Your capital was
returned to you, and your interest was
carried in all the fine wine you would need
to entertain your guests over a lifetime."*

If an investment went bad, you simply threw a very expensive dinner party.

In the mid 2000s, Chinese nouveau riche entered the fine wine market. China's economic growth produced over one million millionaires who sought out Western status symbols. London filled with third-world businessmen who drove Maseratis and shopped at Harrods. New York City received the same treatment, as did luxury brands like Gucci. And fine wine.

The demand for premium wine skyrocketed. Prices saw exponential growth from 2008-2010. Analyses from the London International Vintners Exchange (Liv Ex), a company that tracks fine wine prices like the Dow, show the value of premium wines very gradually increasing in price from 1999 to 2006, then shooting up to over four times the price by 2011.

Whereas premium wines once modestly appreciated in price, suddenly ten thousand dollar cases doubled in price in a year. Hong Kong auctions of Chateau Lafite Rothschild commanded prices at double their traded rates in the United States and Europe days earlier.

Financiers took note. Banks set up fine wine divisions, and wine investment funds began shopping for clients. Liv Ex created its indices for fine wine. The Live Ex 50, which charts the prices of the world's top performing 50 wines, acts exactly like the Nasdaq 500 does for stock brokers. Investors can buy what essentially amount to futures by buying wine "en primeur" before it is bottled.

According to James Maskell, who created Vinetrade, an online marketplace for wines, the Chinese preference for these elite wines is mostly about cachet. Bottles are purchased as a symbol of wealth — or to use as a bribe. Over coffee in San Francisco, Maskell tells us that "the pricing is maybe 25-30% quality, 70-75% brand." Since cachet is all about rarity, demand for a wine (say, a 1982 Mouton Rothschild Bordeaux) increases as supply decreases, accelerating the appreciation of wine prices.

This market consists of very few wines. According to Liv Ex:

> *"The top 25 chateaux in Bordeaux and a handful of properties from other regions dominate. Indeed, our research suggests that just eight wines – the five First Growths, plus Petrus, Cheval Blanc and Ausone – account for more than 80 per cent of a typical wine fund's portfolio by value."*

But investors cannot simply buy top wines and wait for them to appreciate in value. In 2008, Bordeaux producers raised their prices dramatically to capture the profit margins made by speculators. Merchants and investors balked, and suddenly the bubble popped. Investors undercut each other in their hurry to sell. Cases priced at £15,000 sold for £6,000 or £7,000 before the market stabilized.

The top Bordeaux alone cannot satisfy demand, so today's wine investors need to predict the next wine to be anointed a member of this market. Bordeaux second growth wines took off first, then elite French Burgundies. Maskell describes one investor who buys similar Italian wines in the expectation that they too will become elite wines. Wine analysts in London, New York, and Hong Kong, Maskell says, "assemble huge spreadsheets with things like critic scores, drinking windows, available supply and prices that they manually compile and analyse" in search of the next wine that Chinese businessmen will buy to one up each other. They speculate in human snobbery.

Is Wine a Hoax?

Cachet may drive up the price difference between fine wine and table wine. But how great a role do quality differences play? The academic literature on this question appears robust and damning: when tasting wines without reference to their name, type, or price, almost no one can consistently identify them or rate their quality.

In 2007, the California State Fair Commercial Wine Competition named Charles Shaw California's best chardonnay. "It was a delight to taste," announced one judge. In 2012, top French wines (including the premier cru Château Mouton Rothschild) barely defeated wines from New Jersey in a professional tasting. The Jersey wines cost 5% as much as the French wines.

These results are not aberrations. In 2008, a paper in The Journal of Wine Economics found that consumers unaware of a wine's price "on average enjoy more expensive wines slightly less [than cheap ones]." Experts do not fare much better. The study concluded: "In sum, we find a non-negative relationship between price and overall rating for experts. Due to the poor statistical significance of the price coefficient for experts, it remains an open question whether this coefficient is in fact positive." Further academic evidence strongly suggests that experts cannot identify "good" wine.

The 100 point scale for rating wine, invented by Robert M. Parker Jr., is extremely influential.

According to the buying director of prestigious wine merchant BB&R, "Nobody sells wine like Robert Parker. If he turns around and says 2012 is the worst vintage I've tasted, nobody will buy it, but if he says it's the best, everybody will." When retired statistician and hobbyist winemaker Robert Hodgson successfully lobbied to measure the accuracy of the system in the mid 2000s, his results showed that the judging was completely inconsistent. By having the judges rate the same wine multiple times, he found that:

> *"The judges' wine ratings typically varied by ±4 points on a standard ratings scale running from 80 to 100. A wine rated 91 on one tasting would often be rated an 87 or 95 on the next. Some of the judges did much worse, and only about one in 10 regularly rated the same wine within a range of ±2 points."*

Year after year, Hodgson replicated his results. When he broadened his scope to hundreds of wine competitions, he discovered that the distribution of medals "mirrors what might be expected should a gold medal be awarded by chance alone."

More sanguine critics — who do not dismiss studies like Hodgson's as "hogwash" — often point to the short-comings of tastings and the subjectivity of taste. But arguing that judges taste too many wines per tasting, or that the 100 point scale enforces artificial uniformity on subjective tastes, does not seem to address the way these findings shake the foundations of the wine industry.

At the University of Bordeaux, for example, Frederic Broche conducted an experiment in which experienced viniculture students tasted glasses of red and white wine. The students described the red in language typical of reds and the white in language typical of whites. The problem? Both were identical white wines; the "red" had been tinted with food coloring.

So why then do critics and consumers bow down to Lafite Rothschild Bordeaux when objective analysis suggests that the Emperor has no clothes?

Well, outside the world of double-blind taste tests, perceptions matter. People are influenced by wine critics, marketing, and fear of appearing foolish. Another explanation is that big-name labels and high price tags literally make wine taste better. Numerous experiments have shown that people will enjoy a table wine and a fine wine equally if they believe that both are fine wine. The drinkers could be lying about enjoying the "bad" wine due to social pressure. But an experiment involving a Stanford wine tasting group, a lineup of identical wines presented under fake price tags from $5 to $90, and a fMRI machine measuring activity in areas of the brain correlated with pleasure suggests otherwise. Drinking the same wine with a higher price tag did increase pleasure.

Despite the substantial differences in wine production and hundreds of years of history, the most significant determination of a wine's "quality" seems to be pure perception.

A Tale of Two Startups

While the cheap, industrial wine market operates by the same dynamics as the light beer market, fine wine is all about experience — a point aptly demonstrated by the contrasting experiences of two wine business founders.

After a year spent observing wine collectors and investors in London, James Maskell believed that the industry's opaque network of luddite middlemen offered an opportunity. With venture capital backing, he and a co-founder launched a website called Vinetrade in 2012 as a marketplace for buying and selling fine wines. Users could list their wines for sale and buy from other investors and collectors with a few clicks. Maskell and his partner aimed to play a "classic intermediation game — connect buyers and sellers, increase transparency, cut margins, and take a small cut" for themselves.

Customers wanted to avoid fees of around 15% levied by middlemen and to buy and sell without picking up a phone, so many people in the market expected Vinetrade to do well. In early 2013, however, Maskell decided to shut Vinetrade down. The most fundamental problem, he discovered, was that people resisted ordering wine online. For hobbyists, it destroyed the fun of being part of an elite group that unashamedly used words like "tannin" and "subtle." For investors, it denied them the opportunity to exchange information with salesmen. "Even if they don't admit it," Maskell tells us, "people like having the posh voice on the other end of the line. They want reassurance and they want to feel part of the 'boy's club.'"

In the stock market, most assets have an underlying value based on objective facts. In wine, taste and quality is a factor of perception. Investors deal, then, in perceptions of perceptions. In the small world of insanely expensive wine, value and prices are determined by what the wine clique is saying about a given vintage. Sellers could not afford to trade conversations with salesmen for the efficiency of a computer screen because the only currency in the market is everyone else's take on given wines. It would be like trying to predict the next "it" couple in high school without talking to the popular crowd. "I think that we proved that people buying wine don't care about our data and don't care about our graphs," Maskell reflects. "They care about what people are saying."

Two years earlier, Troy Carter took a different approach to a wine startup — he bought a motorcycle and began driving around California wine country. He rode up to small wineries, said, "Hi, I'm Troy," and asked to sample their wines. When he found a wine tasty and unique and the winemaker pleasant and "authentic," he offered to buy wine to distribute and sell through his mailing list "Motorcycle Wineries." Trucks drive the wine he buys from California wineries to his San Francisco warehouse where he distributes them to restaurants and individuals.

Carter's goal with Motorcycle Wineries — other than travelling and tasting any wine he wants — is to bring romance and authenticity to the experience of buying wine. "If you just want wine that tastes good, you can go to Costco," he tells us. "But there is a large group of people that want to have a unique experience. They want to discover wine at a tasting or at a winery off the beaten path. They want the history of finding something that was sitting in a cellar for a long time. That is what I provide."

Carter works only with tiny vineyards that use natural winemaking techniques like organic grapes and follow traditional techniques like hand-bottling. High labor costs renders these wines more expensive. "Authenticity does not scale very well," Carter says. Nevertheless, his bottles cost around $15.

How did Carter convince winemakers to trust him? By wearing leather. "They're the only clothes I own," says Carter, looking down at his understated leather pants and jacket. By showing up on a motorcycle wearing leather, he looked the part of a man who travels the world looking for unique wines. When he didn't wear leather, he was not taken seriously. "Winemakers ride motorcycles," Carter tells us. "I don't know why, but they do. Maybe because they have a romanticized vision of wine. Like I do."

Romancing the Wine Industry

People inside and outside the wine world can argue whether a 1982 Lafite Rothschild is incredible or a scam. But it almost no longer matters. The end result of the fine wine market's cherished romanticization of wines like Lafite is that now only corrupt businessmen and oligarchs can afford it.

Given the way people use the language of wine to police class lines, it's tempting to look at this result with schadenfreude and to cite studies by wine economists as a sign that wine snobs are full of it. For wine insiders, it's easy to retreat to the safety of wine tastings, where the value of fine wine is assumed, and to retort that these studies somehow misunderstand wine. Neither response is quite right.

To discern why, it helps to understand what people mean when they say "taste." Taste buds detect the sweet, sour, bitter, umami, or salty qualities of food and drink, but there is not a sum of each taste that equals the taste of fried chicken or fresh strawberries. Information from all five senses informs our perception of taste.

This is imminently apparent to anyone eating a meal with a cold and sinus congestion; smell and taste are closely linked. The information provided by senses other than our taste buds can make a surprisingly significant impact on how we perceive the taste of wine, and the same is true for other foods and beverages.

Take color, which can trick us into tasting a nonexistent flavor in food in the same way it tricked the wine students tasting white wine dyed red. As the New York Times reports in an article on food coloring:

When tasteless yellow coloring is added to vanilla pudding, consumers say it tastes like banana or lemon pudding. And when mango or lemon flavoring is added to white pudding, most consumers say that it tastes like vanilla pudding. Color creates a psychological expectation for a certain flavor that is often impossible to dislodge.

Sight is crucial to identifying common foods. At Dans Le Noir, a restaurant that employs blind waiters to serve customers expensive dinners in a pitch black restaurant, diners are not told the menu. An investor in the restaurant explains that "After dinner we show them photos of what they ate and the menu, and they can't believe it. They might get the difference between carrots and peas, but they confuse veal and tuna, white and red wine."

There are many other examples of how information garnered from our other senses, including higher-order information, impacts our sense of taste. The surrounding environment makes a difference — we get more pleasure from food when surrounded by soft lighting. So too do our expectations: our experience with similar foods in the past, branding and packaging, and price tags all influence the taste and enjoyment we derive from food and drink.

This means that our enjoyment of good food is just as susceptible to trickery as wine. Fish markets, restaurants, and sushi joints present less expensive fish as their more prestigious (and supposedly better tasting) peers unnoticed every day. This past year, Europeans happily ate up meatballs containing horse meat, only expressing outrage when regulators revealed its presence.

Given the huge variation in wine prices, people react strongly to findings that price has no correlation with pleasure in blind tastings. Yet what these studies really tell us is that our idea of taste as a constant, even if appreciated in subjectively different ways, is a fiction. Due to the complicated way that we experience taste — as an amalgamation of information from all five senses, our expectations, and how we think about what we are tasting — taste is easily manipulated.

True experts are less easily tricked. Master sommeliers have an incredible ability to identify wine; to earn
their certification, they must pass an exam in which
they identify a wine's vintage from a blind tasting. To
see someone with the skill of a master sommelier taste
is a remarkable performance. She recites characteristics of the wine to identify the type of grape, then the
region, and finally the exact vineyard and date of production. Given anecdotes like master French judges
mistaking French and Californian wines, however, the
level of knowledge needed to be immune to trickery is
likely beyond reach of almost the entire market. Even
when they start with substantial industry experience,
aspiring master sommeliers spend years doing nothing
but blind taste tests and studying wine. The majority of
oenophiles who describe wine using pointers they pick
up from wine tasting courses likely appreciate price
tags more than any other qualities of the wine.

While this makes a good case for unapologetically
reaching for bottom shelf wine, this is not necessarily a
reason to shun expensive bottles. Journalist Felix
Salmon points out that while there is no correlation between the price and enjoyment of a wine in blind taste
tests, price and enjoyment almost perfectly correlate
when the price is known. "You can call that Emperor's
New Clothes syndrome if you want," he writes, "but I
like to think that there's something real going on."
Even if it's a con, the effect of liking pricier wine more
is still real; there is no such thing as fake pleasure. According to Salmon, this is why rich people like wine so
much: "It's the most consistently reliable way that they
can convert money into happiness."

But there's a cheaper way to enjoy the con, and that
is to take advantage of all the other factors that "trick"
us into enjoying wine more. Like Troy Carter, you can
ride to Napa and walk the vineyards before you buy a

bottle. If you don't live near wine country, you can talk to the manager of a wine store about the wines she loves. A nice pair of wine glasses, candles, and a picnic in a beautiful park all lend wine a refined air.

All these strategies take advantage of the psychological biases that lead us to enjoy the same wine more than we would in other circumstances. And they do so without the rarefied price tag.

PART II:
EXISTING POWER STRUCTURES

"They want me to stand with them, right? But where the fuck they at when they supposed to be standing by us? I mean, when the shit goes bad and there's hell to pay, where they at? This game is rigged, man. We like the little bitches on a chessboard."

(Bodie, *The Wire*)

6.

THE TYRANNY OF
TAXI MEDALLIONS

The life of a taxi driver is hard. When cabbies start a shift, they owe about $100 to their company as payment just for the opportunity to drive a taxi. They might not break even until halfway through their shift, or maybe not at all that day. In most American cities, they have to work very long hours to make a living.

During a shift, taxi drivers play a strange form of roulette when they pick up anonymous customers. The customer could be a pleasant family that tips them well, a drunk college kid that vomits in their car, or a violent criminal that robs and assaults them. After the customer leaves the car, there is no record of their behavior in the taxi.

Why is it that taxi drivers have to pay their companies for the privilege of doing a difficult and dangerous job? After all, when you show up to your office, you don't pay a fee to your boss every morning.

The reason taxi drivers have to pay for the right to work is that they need access to a taxi medallion. A medallion is a permit issued by the government that is required to drive a cab in most American cities. If you don't use the medallion yourself, you can rent it out to other drivers on your own or, more commonly, through a taxi company. Taxi companies that rent out access to the medallions have immense economic power over the drivers. If you're not willing to basically become an in-dentured servant to get medallion access, well, you're out of luck.

Taxi medallions are scarce, which is what makes them powerful. It also makes them expensive; medal-lions can sell for hundreds of thousands of dollars on secondary markets. In most American cities, there is a hard cap on the number of permits issued. That num-ber doesn't change for years or even decades. This scarcity of medallions is also the reason it's so hard to find a taxi in many American cities (cough, cough: San Francisco).

But what if you didn't need a taxi medallion in order to drive people around in exchange for money? A num-ber of startups are doing just that, pioneering a move-ment called "ride-sharing" where drivers are typically just regular members of the community driving their own cars around in exchange for money.

If anyone with access to a car and cell phone app could become a driver, what would happen to today's taxi drivers, the owners of medallions, and the industry that exists to extract value from the scarcity of the medallions?

Taxi Medallions 101

The current structure of the American taxi industry began in New York City when "taxi medallions" were introduced in the 1930s. Taxis were extremely popular in the city, and the government realized it needed to make sure drivers weren't psychopaths luring victims into their cars. So, New York City required cabbies to apply for a taxi medallion license. Given the technology available in the 1930s, it was a reasonable solution to the taxi safety problem, and other cities soon followed suit. (Many of them have different names for the licenses, but we'll refer to them all as medallions.)

But the taxi medallion requirement had an unintended consequence — it made taxis scarce. The "right" to drive a taxi became very valuable as demand outstripped supply. When this medallion system was introduced in New York City in 1937, there were 11,787 issued. That number remained constant until 2004. Today there are 13,150.

As demand for taxis has increased while supply remained relatively fixed, the cost of medallions in New York City has skyrocketed to over one million dollars. In Boston, the price of a medallion is $625,000. In San Francisco, you need to drive a taxi at least 10 hours a week if you want to hold a medallion and lease it out. Veteran taxi drivers can sell their medallions for $300,000, and the city of San Francisco takes a $100,000 commission on the sale.

In the taxi market, there are three players: The medallion holders who have the ordained right from the government to operate a taxi, the taxi driver who pays the medallion holder to drive the taxi, and, sitting in between these two parties, the taxi dispatch company. A pure middleman, the dispatch company facilitates the transmission of funds between medallion holders and provides some infrastructure like scheduling, fleet maintenance, and occasional customer leads for the taxis.

There is some overlap between these three entities. Sometimes drivers own medallions, or taxi companies hold medallions. Still, it's useful to isolate these three main economic interests in the taxi industry. How each of them reacts to industry disruption is very different.

The Taxing Days of Taxi Drivers

In America, we often complain about taxis. They're never around when it's raining, they don't show up when you need to get to the airport, the interiors are filthy, and the drivers talk on the phone and drive aggressively. But as bad as consumers have it, the taxi drivers have it worse.

The root cause of taxi drivers' problems is that they need access to a medallion in order to drive and make a living. Because of this, taxi companies that distribute medallion access can charge usurious fees and freely abuse the drivers. If the drivers don't like it, well, then they can't be taxi drivers.

In a study of Los Angeles taxi drivers, UCLA professors Gary Blasi and Jacqueline Leavitt found that taxi drivers work on average 72 hours a week for a median take home wage of $8.39 per hour. Not only do they have to pay $2,000 in "leasing fees" per month to taxi companies, but the city regulates things like what color socks they can wear (black) and how many days a week they can go to the airport (once). None of the drivers in the survey had health insurance provided by their companies and 61% of them were completely without health insurance.

Recently, the Boston Globe published an undercover exposé on the Boston taxi industry. One of the Globe's writers (who used to drive a cab in college) started driving a taxi for a company called Boston Cab. He discovered a corrupt system where medallion access empowered taxi dispatchers to abuse drivers.

The writer describes the fees drivers faced as follows:

> *"Boston Cab charges him the standard shift rate of $77, plus an $18 premium for a newer cab, as well as a city-sanctioned,*

*30-cent parking violation fee. Factor in the
sales tax ($5.96) and optional collision
damage waiver ($5), and his cost per shift
is $106.26, not including gas."*

In order to get the opportunity to pay this $106 fee,
taxi drivers had to bribe the dispatchers to get good
shifts or to drive at all. The author waited around for
hours before he could drive a taxi since he didn't bribe
the dispatchers.

On top of the base fees the driver owed the taxi company for each day of work, the taxi company would
arbitrarily make up fees that drivers needed to pay. In
the Globe reporter's case:

*"After every shift, the reporter fills his gas
tank at a station less than three blocks
away.*

*He pumps until the gas gurgles over onto
his shoes. Yet when he reaches the garage
one night, the gas attendant tells him he
owes the company an additional $2.09.*

*'How is that possible?' the driver asks the
attendant, incredulously.*

*'It happens to everyone,' the attendant
shrugs."*

Passengers often complain that they feel unsafe in a
taxi with an aggressive driver. But the drivers are the
ones who have to worry about safety. According to the
Bureau of Labor Statistics, driving a taxi is one of the
top ten jobs that result in work related fatalities. The

odds of taxi drivers dying because of work related fatality is even higher than for police officers. Picking up anonymous strangers who could be violent late at night while carrying a lot of cash is risky. Just sharing the road with other drivers is risky too. In the case of the Boston Globe undercover driver, he (and his passengers) ended up in the hospital when a drunk driver ran a red light and crashed into his car.

Medallions require that drivers get permission from someone else to drive a cab. This power asymmetry gives the medallion-holders a lot of leverage over drivers, and it appears that they abuse it.

And Here Comes Disruption

A number of mobile phone apps, however, are replacing taxi dispatch services and allowing anyone with a car to become a taxi driver without needing access to a medallion. Increasingly, if you want to become a taxi driver, all you need is a car and an app that tells you where to pick up passengers.

In the last half decade, two trends conspired to end the taxi medallion regime. First, people are more comfortable with trusting strangers. This is evidenced by the success of the company AirBnB, which allows regular people people to rent out extra rooms in their home to strangers. Marketplaces like AirBnB provide the data (reviews of guests and hosts), brand, and insurance that allow strangers to trust each other.

The second trend is that we all carry around location enabled sensors in our pockets in the form of our phones. Before smart phones, the best way to find a taxi was to go outside and wait for one on the street like an idiot. Now, you can click a button and an app that knows your location can connect you with the nearest car. Since you can see reviews of the driver, you can trust that it's safe to get in the car.

The ride-sharing economy started conservatively with Uber allowing anyone to call a black town car via its app. That quickly led to companies like Sidecar and Lyft, which let anyone with a car act as a taxi driver, and hybrid services like InstantCab that let taxi drivers and community drivers both get fares. These companies and their products are called "ride-sharing" apps.

Cheekily, if you hail a ride using one of these ride-sharing apps, the payment is often called a "donation." This sort of seems like a made up legal loophole that can justify any behavior ("Officer I wasn't paying for sex, I was making a donation!"). But for now that's one of the ways ride-sharing apps nominally get around local regulations that restrict who can be a taxi.

The Advantage of the Ride-Sharing Apps

Another significant way ride-sharing apps avoid taxi medallion legislation is by not picking people up from the street. You have to hail them using an app. This ends up being a feature, rather than a constraint. First, it's safer for the driver and the passenger because the transaction isn't anonymous. Second, it's more reliable than a taxi dispatched by a cab company. We spoke to InstantCab CEO Aarjav Trivedi to understand why:

> *"Cab drivers don't have to listen to cab company dispatch and rarely do. If they see people with their bags that look like they're going to the airport by the side of the road, they will ditch the dispatched call and pick up the street hail. They have no reason to be accountable to the cab company, which in turn has no reason to be accountable to customers because the company makes practically all their money by leasing cabs and medallions to*

*drivers. That's why taxis dispatched by
cab companies don't show up when you
call them."*

InstantCab is in an interesting position because it
has taxis and community drivers in its fleet. However,
if a taxi driver bails on an InstantCab customer to pick
up someone on the street instead, he gets booted from
the service. InstantCab has to artificially add this constraint to taxi drivers, otherwise its service wouldn't
work for the customer.

Finally, these apps can use technology to help drivers optimize their earnings. Taxi drivers maximize
profit by knowing where the demand will be depending
on the hour and timing where they look for fares ac-
cordingly. Over time, some drivers develop an intuition
about this. Ride-sharing apps have the data to formal-
ize and optimize this learning. In a world without data,
it would take taxi drivers years to know exactly where
in these high demand zones they need to be and when
they should be there. If it's 5 pm, should they be in
front of JP Morgan or Zynga? If it's midnight, should
they be at the Ruby Skye nightclub or Circa? Mastering
these skills takes years and is essential to making a
good living as a taxi driver.

In San Francisco, the transformation from a medallion constrained taxi system to a free market is nearly
complete. When Uber recently announced its latest
round of funding in June 2014, it noted that its revenue
in San Francisco was now more than the entire legacy
taxi industry in the city. These ride-sharing companies
are all rapidly expanding across the world.

The Winners and Losers of Disruption

If this post-medallion system is allowed to flourish, the
medallion holders and dispatchers will be out of

business.

The value of a medallion drops to almost zero because anyone can be a community driver without one. The extent to which they retain any value is the extent to which drunk people continue stumbling out of bars and hailing a cab without using their phones. So, medallion holders speculated in holding a government asset and lost. Some of these people are also taxi drivers or operators of taxi dispatch companies. Like Greek bondholders, they gambled and lost big.

The middleman in this current system, the taxi dispatch company, will be eviscerated. The software of Uber, Sidecar, Lyft, and InstantCab dispatches rides to customers, the ride-sharing companies provide insurance, and the drivers provide their own car maintenance. We doubt that the dispatchers will be missed. They have the power to mistreat drivers, and it seems like they exercise that power freely.

Taxi drivers working for these apps reap a number of benefits. They no longer get nailed with opaque fees or start the day hundreds of dollars in debt, so they can start making money the second they start driving. Picking up customers now that cabbies have their credit cards on file is safer because they have a record of everyone entering their taxis. Finally, they are so far making more money per hour than under the medallion system. Most ride-sharing app companies advertise that you can make $20-$30 per hour, which is much better than the current $10 an hour taxi drivers make.

So are taxi drivers better off in a liberated, medallion free system? It depends. They will face more competition because anyone can become a taxi driver. Despite increased competition, however, taxi drivers might thrive in a new world where fees are less onerous. Aarjav Trivedi of InstantCab points out another nuance that helps cab drivers:

"Drivers are in two camps. The Opportunist who is doing it for extra money and the Pro who has been doing it day in day out for years, perhaps because of their experience as a professional driver.

The Pro always wins: they can pick up and drop off customers faster, do a lot more runs, and get paid more. Their knowledge and intuition have evolved to remember how to navigate streets better and where demand is going to be at a certain time."

According to Trivedi, professional drivers are slaughtering amateur community drivers in terms of take home pay. The drivers that know what they're doing (professionals) and can afford to buy or lease their owns cars may be able to make a very good living under this system. The opportunists might not.

What should taxi drivers do to ride out this disruption? The best bet is probably to try out a few shifts on a ride-sharing app. They can drive around on Lyft or Sidecar with their personal car or on Uber with either their taxi or personal car and see what happens.

If drivers find they like getting customers from ride-sharing apps and can make more money, it's time to leave the sinking ship of the medallion-based taxi economy. If they find they make less money, it's probably in taxi drivers' best interest to join medallion-holders and taxi companies in their pursuit to block ride-sharing apps from spreading across America.

What Will the Government Do?

Ed Reiskin, Director of the San Francisco Municipal Transportation Agency, has made his thoughts on the taxi issue clear. "These medallions are public assets," he told *The San Francisco Chronicle* in 2012. "The value belongs to the people of San Francisco for the benefit of the transportation system."

It seems like it's a safe bet that no one who uses mass transport in San Francisco actually considers medallions to be a public asset. The people who view medallions as a public asset are the beneficiaries of the current system: medallion holders, taxi companies insulated from competition, and, most likely, public officials whose job it is to dole out medallions.

A public asset is safe, efficient transportation, not a scarcity of taxis. Medallions were created in the 1930s to make sure taxis were safe. Regulation of the ridesharing industry needs to focus on safety by making it easy to run background checks on drivers and report driver reviews and incidents to municipal authorities. Right now, all the startups are very focused on having safe drivers because they're under public scrutiny. But ten years from now, less scrupulous companies may emerge.

The second area where government can help is by protecting drivers from platform lock-in. Right now drivers can only work for one ride-sharing app. The company you drive for is responsible for 100% of your earnings — a level of control that could be abused. If regulators want to help consumers and drivers, they should mandate that a driver cannot be locked into one ride-sharing platform. A driver should be able to freely get a pickup call from Uber, Lyft or whomever. More competition between the ridesharing apps is good for drivers and good for consumers.

It seems as if taxi medallion holders and taxi dis-

patch companies will get wiped out. If local governments step in and ban ridesharing apps, it will be to
protect these interests at everyone else's expense. So
far, it seems like that's what many local governments
are doing: banning ride-sharing apps.

Those that benefit from the taxi medallion system
have been protected for 80 years. In that time, they
abused taxi drivers and produced a crappy product.
Ride-sharing apps should be allowed to take over the
market — until they too are disrupted by self-driving
cars. And so it goes.

7.

BEING REALLY, REALLY, RIDICULOUSLY GOOD LOOKING

"I'm pretty sure there's a lot more to life than being really, really, ridiculously good looking. And I plan on finding out what that is."
(Derek Zoolander, Zoolander)

Humans like attractive people. Those blessed with the leading man looks of Brad Pitt or the curves of Beyonce can expect to make, on average, 10% to 15% more money over the course of their career than their more homely friends. Without being consciously aware that they are doing it, people consistently assume that good-looking people are friendly, successful, and trustworthy. They also assume that unattractive people are unfriendly, unsuccessful, and dishonest. It pays to be good looking.

This insight is not lost on Madison Avenue or Hollywood. This is why every beer commercial features an attractive woman and Scarlett Johansson endorses products ranging from perfume to soda makers. This is also why companies hire beautiful women to stand in trade show booths and Abercrombie & Fitch badgers attractive customers into applying for sales positions.

Consumers associate the perceived positive characteristics of attractive people with their products and companies.

The good-looking sales associates at Abercrombie & Fitch may sell more clothes, but is that legal? Surely there must be some controls to ensure that unattractive people are not excluded from large swaths of the labor market. So what protections exist for those of us without smooth skin and thin waists?

The surprising answer is none. America has no law preventing companies from using attractiveness as a hiring criteria, regardless of whether the job is exotic dancer, salesman, or software engineer. It's more or less acceptable from a legal standpoint to discriminate based on looks in America. Is that a problem?

The Science of Beauty

Beauty is often considered subjective and "in the eye of the beholder."

To some extent this is true. People argue over the attractiveness of various celebrities precisely because differences of opinion exist. Tastes also vary by time and place. Victorian England admired pale skin. During the Colonial Era, men showed off their calves like men display their biceps today. And skinniness has not always been considered the ideal.

Academic work on beauty, however, finds that much of what we find attractive is consistent over time and across cultures. In general, people find symmetry and averageness of facial features attractive.

When images of perfectly symmetrical faces are created in Photoshop, people prefer them over their unsymmetrical counterparts. The same is true of photos created by merging many faces to get a composite. Scientists speculate that we prefer symmetry and average features because they (at least at some point) indicated healthy genes or other evolutionary advantages.

More evidence of a universal, objective basis for beauty comes from studies of babies presented with pictures of different faces. The pictures the babies gazed at the longest were consistently the ones rated as most attractive by panels of adults.

The Halo Effect

In the early 20th century, psychologist Edward Thorndike noticed that psychologists' evaluations of very different traits in the same individual seemed suspiciously consistent. He suspected that a bias was to blame.

To test his finding, he asked military officers to rate their subordinates on characteristics such as neatness, physique, leadership skills, intellect, and loyalty. He again found that the results were too consistent. When officers rated a soldier especially high for one quality, they tended to rate him high in other areas where he did not excel. Soldiers rated especially poor in one area also received poor marks across the board. The officers' opinion of their soldiers for one characteristic dominated their overall impression.

Thorndike called this the "halo effect." Researchers have documented its influence in many situations, including the halo effect of physical attractiveness. As psychologist Robert Cialdini writes in his bestselling book Influence, "We automatically assign to good-looking individuals such favorable traits as talent, kindness, honesty, and intelligence." Within the business world, he says, attractive people benefit from the halo effect in two major ways.

The first is that we tend to "comply with those we like." This is why magazine offers from neighborhood children are so irresistible and "Tupperware parties" (where mothers host parties to sell Tupperware to their friends) are so successful. It's also why Joe Girard, one of the most successful car salesmen of all time, sent all of his customers holiday cards with the phrase "I like you" every year. Likeable people have an easier time selling products, and attractive people are eminently likeable due to the halo effect.

The second is that we tend to associate people with the products they sell and companies they represent. Cialdini points out that weathermen are blamed (by otherwise rational people) for storms and that the Persian Empire either killed messengers or treated them as heroes depending on the nature of the news they brought. (An example of the literal origins of the phrase "Don't kill the messenger.") The use of association in advertising and sales is so powerful that it works even when people are perfectly aware of companies' intent. Cialdini writes:

> *"In one study, men who saw a new-car ad that included a seductive young woman model rated the car as faster, more appealing, more expensive-looking, and better designed than did men who viewed the same ad without the model. Yet when asked later, the men refused to believe that the presence of the young woman had influenced their judgments."*

In combination, these two principles and the halo effect give attractive people a huge advantage in any job that involves interaction with customers, business partners, or the general public. A good-looking spokesperson is more likely to be trusted and imbue his company with a positive image. Beautiful saleswomen can more easily close deals. Sources are more likely to trust beautiful journalists and confide sensitive stories to handsome reporters.

People recognize, tolerate, and even encourage the practice of hiring attractive people as actors and models. But the same principle that allows Jennifer Garner to do a better job selling makeup than the average girl next door is also at work in a huge number of professions.

The Best Looking Sales Staff in the Land

Although it is a clothing store, Abercrombie & Fitch is not necessarily famous for its clothes. The company brand ties attractive people and pop culture. In its stores, pop music blares, perfume hangs in the air, and attractive sales staff use catch phrases like "Hey! What's up?" Pictures on the wall feature models' six pack abs more than actual clothing.

Abercrombie & Fitch unapologetically hires only the most attractive applicants. Recruiters seek out beautiful people in stores, on the street, and at fraternities and sororities. Its codified "Look Policy" so prioritizes appearance that managers reportedly throw applications from unattractive job seekers into the trash. The company's rebranding from an ailing athletics apparel store — purchased for $47 million in 1988 — to a retailer of preppy clothing staffed by "models" helped it earn $4.5 billion in revenue in 2013.

In 2004, fourteen individuals launched a class action lawsuit against Abercrombie & Fitch that described its Look Policy as discriminatory. Their lawyers argued that a certain look was not central to the essence of A&F's business and the actual job of answering questions about polo shirts.

But Abercrombie & Fitch was not in trouble for hiring only hotties — the company was charged with racism. The plaintiffs noted that A&F's policy of favoring a "natural, classic American style" translated to a "virtually all white" sales staff and relegating minority employees to positions in the back room. A&F settled for $50 million and agreed to change their Look Policy.

Even if they had wanted to, the plaintiffs could not have accused A&F of appearance-based discrimination or "lookism." There is no federal law against it. Companies can use attractiveness as a basis for employment decisions in all but several American cities that have passed legislation against it. This is true regardless of whether attractiveness is central to the occupation (a stripper or actor), a branding or sales strategy (Abercrombie & Fitch's sales staff), or completely irrelevant (personal assistant or software engineer). When a lawsuit does challenge appearance-based policies, it draws instead on laws that ban discrimination on the basis of race, gender, age, or disability.

The most common lawsuits challenge companies that hire only attractive women on the basis of gender discrimination since this would exclude men and place obligations (in terms of dressing seductively) on female but not male employees. Like the A&F case, these law-suits draw on Title VII of the Civil Rights Act, which "prohibits employment discrimination based on race, color, religion, sex and national origin." The law is strict: Companies must prove that their employment practices constitute a "bona fide occupational qualifi-cation" that is necessary for the essence of the business.

A strip club can claim that seductive women are the essence of its business; restaurants and airlines cannot claim the same defense. In the seventies, Southwest Airlines marketed itself as the "love" airline by hiring only attractive female stewardesses who dressed in hot pants. (They also called check-in counters "quickie machines.") But in 1981, a man denied a job with Southwest sued the company for sexual discrimination. Southwest began hiring male employees after the judge ruled that the company's purpose was not "forthrightly to titillate and entice male customers." Even Hooters, the restaurant chain whose entire premise is for hot, scantily clad women to serve men buffalo wings, fell victim to the law. It has kept the "Hooter Girls" mainly by settling lawsuits out of court, but it has opened more staff positions to men and women that do not require good looks.

In more theoretical discussions, lawyers argue that the Age Discrimination in Employment Act could be used to challenge appearance-based discrimination in which age plays a role. Even more theoretically, they speculate that the interpretation of the Americans With Disabilities Act, while not originally intended to protect people lacking perfect, tanned bodies, could be extended to include attractiveness.

But in practice, as long as a company is open to hiring attractive people of every gender, race, creed, and age, it is free to hire and promote staff the same way fraternity boys play hot or not. Despite the legal sanction, Abercrombie & Fitch continues to seek out attractive applicants — whether black, Asian, Indian, or Hispanic — and attract controversy for doing so.

Do Women Benefit As Well?

While the halo effect has been demonstrated to help attractive people in many personal and professional settings, the bias doesn't always help women in their careers.

A 2010 study, for example, examined how attractiveness benefitted men and women in different jobs. Attractive men had an advantage over their plain peers across the board. But for jobs considered "masculine," such as mechanical engineer, construction supervisor, and even director of finance, women actually paid a penalty for being attractive.

A separate experiment that sent out identical applications with and without pictures, however, found that attractive women fared worse than "plain-looking" women regardless of industry. But it theorized that attractive women faced a penalty because human resources offices are staffed mainly by women. If a mostly male or evenly balanced staff reviewed the applications, attractive women may have enjoyed an advantage.

Results like this suggest that women may not benefit from attractiveness as much as men, or may even suffer reverse appearance-based discrimination depending on the circumstances.

A Skin Deep World

While it's not the subject of congressional committees and headline news, some debate exists over whether appearance-based hiring policies should be considered discrimination, effectively offering unattractive people similar protections to those that exist for women, minorities, senior citizens, and the disabled. Without equating the disadvantages faced by plain-looking people to the injustices minorities face, advocates insist that this would also seek a society that is merit-based and where people are not limited by physical appearance.

Many people despise Abercrombie & Fitch for hiring only good-looking staff, but Harvard economist Robert Barro argues that good looks are a legitimate aspect of productive economic activity. "A worker's physical appearance, to the extent that it is valued by customers and co-workers," he writes in an editorial, "is as legitimate a job qualification as intelligence, dexterity, job experience, and personality." Intelligence is doled out unequally and determines which jobs people can and cannot get, yet we do not ask the government to intervene.

The two sides argue over other practical issues:

Could the government accurately judge when attractiveness is irrelevant to a job? Would legal protection unleash a wave frivolous lawsuits? More importantly, critics point out that unattractive individuals have not been discriminated against historically the way that minorities and women have — a justification for legal intervention. Yet just as legislation aims to protect women, minorities, and the elderly from the consequences of irrational biases — women can't be good executives, for example, or black men and women are less intelligent — unattractive people are constantly on the losing side of irrational biases.

Company policies that favor attractive staff may seem defensible for jobs where the halo effect means that a worker's looks will benefit the business. But companies seem to favor attractive employees even when looks are irrelevant.

In an experiment run by Harvard and Wesleyan professors, for example, participants performed a task in which beauty was of no help. Other participants acted as their bosses and set their compensation — either blindly or while aware of their attractiveness. Mirroring real world findings, attractive participants earned wages 12% to 17% higher. Yet, as the researchers wrote, the lion's share of the wage gap was explained by how "employers (wrongly) expect good-looking workers to perform better than their less attractive counterparts." This suggests that attractive people enjoy advantages even in fields like software engineering or corporate management where their looks don't benefit the business.

Beauty is just as irrationally beneficial in the supposedly egalitarian setting of a courtroom. Researchers tracking the outcomes of court cases find that attractive (and guilty) defendants receive lighter sentences. In another experiment where participants decided how much money to award the victim of a negligence case, they awarded the victim almost twice as much if he or she was more attractive than the defendant. Justice is not blind.

In stories, villains are usually ugly and the heroes are good-looking. We expect the same in life. Children and adults alike associate physical attractiveness and height with strength, intelligence, and goodness and associate ugliness with corresponding character flaws. Studies of schoolchildren find that teachers view misbehavior by a good-looking child as less naughty. Teachers also assume that attractive children are more intelligent than their less-attractive peers. One educator notes that this can "become a self-fulfilling prophecy: teachers expect better looking kids to outperform in school and devote more attention to children who are perceived to have greater potential."

Personally and professionally, the halo effect of attractiveness shapes people's lives in ways that go far beyond people holding the door for a pretty girl. And unlike the case of an actress's stunning looks propelling her to stardom, it often operates subconsciously. Good-looking people earn more money, are judged more positively, and even receive more lenient treatment in court than their plainer looking counterparts.

We're told not to judge a book by its cover. But we do. All the time. And everyone's life is affected by it.

8.

DO ELITE COLLEGES DISCRIMINATE AGAINST ASIANS?

Applying to colleges in the United States is a stressful, competitive process. In 1970, the acceptance rate at Stanford University was 22.4%; today, only 5.1% of applicants are accepted into the school. Across the country, top schools like Harvard, MIT and Yale are reporting record-low acceptance rates. The number of students applying to elite colleges is exploding, and those applicants have better test scores than ever. It's never been harder to get into a selective university.

Asian-American students face an extra source of stress: deciding whether to respond to the application question asking for their race and ethnicity. True or not, there is a perception that Asians are at a disadvantage in the college admissions process. Asian students going through the process related their experiences to USA Today:

> *"I didn't want to put 'Asian' down...*
> *because my mom told me there's*
> *discrimination against Asians in the*
> *application process... Not to really*
> *generalize, but a lot of Asians, they have*

*perfect SATs, perfect GPAs, ... so it's hard
to let them all in.*

*As someone who was applying with
relatively strong scores, I didn't want to be
grouped into that stereotype... I didn't
want to be written off as one of the 1.4
billion Asians that were applying."*

Are these fears justified? Is it statistically more
difficult to be accepted into a top university if you are
Asian? Ivy League colleges deny this to be true, but
what does the data say?

Statistical Evidence of Discrimination

Those who contend that selective colleges discriminate
against Asians point to three main sources of data.

First, some top colleges have in the past (though not
recently) released detailed admissions data. Second, in
1996, California banned state universities from considering race and ethnicity in admissions decisions. The
result is a natural experiment where you can see what
happens to the number of Asians accepted before and
after this decision. Finally, researchers have tried to
quantify whether the number of high performing
Asians has been increasing and whether that has corre-
sponded to more placements in selective schools.

The most cited, well-researched evidence that it's
harder for Asians to get into top colleges is presented
by Princeton professor Thomas Espenshade and his
collaborator Alexandria Radford in their 2009 book,
No Longer Separate, Not Yet Equal. In this book, the
researchers analyzed the complete application histories
of eight "elite" universities in 1997 (the last year these
schools released this information). While the data is
over 15 years old, it's the most complete dataset

publicly available.

Espenshade and Radford use the 1997 data to show the overall acceptance rates by race and class at public and private universities with highly selective admissions criteria. According to their data, at private schools Asians have an 18.4% acceptance rate versus 25.7% for whites, 26.7% for Hispanics, and 31.0% for blacks.

The authors find that being Asian instead of white is the equivalent of a 140 point score penalty on your SAT when applying to top private universities. For example, a white student that scored 1360 on the SAT would be on equal footing with an Asian student that scored 1500. Asian applicants have 67% lower odds of admission than white applicants with comparable test scores.

Ultimately, Espenshade and Radford come short of making any conclusions about whether Asians are discriminated against. Their data indicates that Asians needed higher standardized test scores than whites to get accepted to top schools in 1997, but this doesn't consider other parts of a "holistic" admissions process such as athletic prowess, legacy status (being the child of an alum), or quality of admissions essays and recommendation letters.

The next piece of evidence frequently cited in the debate is the admissions data of public universities in California (Berkeley, UCLA, UCSD, Davis, etc). In 1996, it became illegal for these schools to consider race in their admissions criteria. This created a natural experiment showing what happens to the number of Asian students at a school when admissions officers are not allowed to consider that they are Asian.

Since these are state universities, the admissions data, which includes the race of students, is publicly available. Let's consider the data for UC Berkeley, the most prestigious and selective public university in California. Over the past 25 years, the percentage of Asian students accepted into UC Berkeley has exploded from 25% (1989) to 45% (2014).

While this is interesting, it's not necessarily proof that Asians were discriminated against prior to the 1996 ruling. If the number of college-aged Asians rose dramatically during this time period, it would be natural that more Asians are accepted at Berkeley today.

So let's look at what has happened to the acceptance rate over time. Did it get easier for Asians to get in after admissions officers could no longer consider students' ethnicity? Of course, it's gotten a lot harder for everyone to get in over the last 25 years, so let's compare the Asian acceptance rate to the acceptance rate for everyone else at Berkeley.

In 1989, Asians had a 31% acceptance rate at UC Berkeley versus a more generous 44% rate for non-Asians. It was a lot harder for Asians to get into Berkeley than for non-Asians. By 2012, the opposite was true — acceptance rates for Asians became 21% versus 16% for all other races.

Finally, the fact that the growth in the Asian population has not been reflected in their numbers at top schools is also cited. Not only have the number of college-aged Asians increased in the last two decades, but the number of academically high performing Asians has as well. This viewpoint is summarized quantitatively by Ron Unz, founder of The American Conservative — a publication that is quite vocal about this issue.

The data Unz has compiled shows that while the number of college aged Asians has increased dramatically, Asians' presence at top schools has shrunk or remained flat. By contrast, CalTech, which has a strictly race-neutral admissions policy, has kept pace with the growth in the Asian population (this is also true of the school we previously examined).

Unz also contends that you should see a lot more Asians at Ivy League schools during this time, because they were kicking ass and taking names academically. Asians now make up 58% of the US Math Olympiad winners, 75% of the of the Computing Olympiad winners, and 64% of the finalists for the Science Talent Search — percentages 3-5 times higher than they were for Asians in the 1980s.

According to standardized tests and talent competitions, there is strong evidence that Asian Americans aren't just doing pretty well — they're completely dominating.

The Counter Argument

"Harvard welcomes talented students from all backgrounds, including Asian-Americans... The admissions committee does not use quotas."
(Jeff Neil, Harvard University Communications Department)

It's hard to find evidence that contradicts what's presented above. While the data is either stale or limited, all of it indicates that Asians are under-represented at top schools. At the same time, admissions officers vigorously deny that there is any bias against Asian Americans. Moreover, this author knows former admissions officers and they're all really nice people. It's very hard to imagine them hatching dastardly plots to keep Asians from their schools.

The gist of the argument that top schools don't discriminate against Asians is that academic qualifications are only one of the many criteria used in a "holistic" admissions process. There are so many students with great academic qualifications relative to the spots available that academic qualifications almost don't matter for serious candidates. Given that so many students meet the minimum academic criteria (which are high), successful applicants need to contribute more than just brain power to their school of choice.

This viewpoint is crystallized by Rod Bugarin, former member of Brown and Columbia admissions committees:

> *"Yes, if you considered only test scores,*
> *Asian and Asian-American students would*
> *seem to be at a disadvantage. But the*
> *students who rise to the top of the highly*
> *personal and subjective admissions*
> *process are those who have submitted the*
> *strongest comprehensive applications."*

The unstated implication of this quote is that while Asians have high test scores, the rest of their applications, on average, are deficient in some manner.

The next argument is that top schools aren't actually biased against Asians, but rather biased against people that aren't athletes or children of alumni. In 1990, the US Office of Civil Rights concluded an investigation into whether Harvard discriminated against Asians. The commission concluded that most of the under representation could be explained by the fact that few Asians were recruited athletes, or children of alumni.

This might explain why the number of Asians at Harvard was relatively low in 1990, but it doesn't explain why that number is still about the same after two decades of growth in the Asian share of America's population.

Finally, there are those who argue that the "Asian discrimination question" is merely being used as a "wedge issue" to overturn affirmative action and lower the number of blacks, hispanics, and historically under-represented minorities on campus. While this is a valid concern, it evades the question of whether Asians are held to a different academic standard than the baseline group (whites). That's the question we're focusing on.

Reading the universities' responses to accusations of an anti-Asian bias in admission decisions is frustrating because they don't provide any data to back their refutations. They simply state that there is no discrimination today. They refuse to even release recent admissions data in order to refute the old and stale data that suggests Asians have to score much higher on the SATs than whites in order to be accepted into college.

Holistic admissions policies, as they stand today, are a subjective black box that could be used for any purpose — good or evil, inclusion or exclusion. In absence of providing any data, Ivy League admissions offices are saying, "Trust us, we use our power for good." But how have universities used this power in the past? Are they really worthy of trust?

A History of Discrimination

Colleges in the United States likely think of themselves as progressive institutions. They have forward-thinking faculties, a stated objective of inclusion, and commitments to public service. This author might even personally think they are wonderful, progressive places. But no generation ever thinks of itself as being racist or discriminatory, even when they are. If the data suggests you're discriminating against a group, and you're forced to come up with qualitative, opaque explanations for why the discrepancy exists, historically, that has been a bad sign.

Has the Ivy League, for example, proven itself as an institution that should be given the benefit of the doubt over accusations of discrimination? Schools in the Ivy League have been around for almost 400 years. For the vast majority of that time, women, blacks, or anyone other than white men were not allowed to attend. During this period, the educators, admissions officers, and alumni undoubtedly considered themselves a part of great institutions bringing light to the world, but the hindsight of history proves they had racist and sexist admissions policies.

Holistic admissions criteria emerged at Ivy League schools in the early 20th century and were almost immediately twisted for virulently anti-semitic purposes. Until the 1920s, students took an admissions test and those that did well on the test were admitted to the colleges "almost entirely on the basis of academic criteria." This resulted in lots of Jewish men on Harvard, Princeton, and Yale campuses.

An alumni visiting the Harvard campus around this time was shocked by the scene:

> *"Naturally, after 25 years, one expects to find many changes, but to find that one's University had become so Hebrewized was a fearful shock. There were Jews to the right of me, Jews to the left of me, in fact they were so obviously everywhere that instead of leaving the yard with pleasant memories of the past I left with a feeling of utter disgust of the present and grave doubts about the future of my Alma Mater."*

It's around this time that Ivy League schools switched from a strictly quantitative system of test scores to a more subjective, holistic approach. The holistic approach was used to squelch diversity and the number of Jews in American universities then plummeted. After these "reforms," the percentage of Jews at Harvard declined from 27.6% to 17.1%; Columbia saw a dip from 32.7% to 14.6%. During this time period, the percentage of Jews attending Cornell University's medical school dropped from 40.0% to 3.6%; similarly, at Boston University's medical school, this number dropped from 48.4% to 12.5%.

The concept of giving preference to legacy of alumni also started to gain prominence. This admission practice was created at Yale in 1925 and allowed admission officers there to admit 'Yale sons of good character and reasonably good record,' rather than more academically qualified candidates.

As late as the 1950s, prominent administrators at Harvard and Yale publicly commented on the appearance of the kind of students they sought. David Brooks of *The New York Times* summarizes:

> *"Paul Buck argued in several essays that Harvard did not want to become dominated by the 'sensitive, neurotic boy,' by those who are 'intellectually over-stimulated.' Instead, he said, Harvard should be seeking out boys who are of the 'healthy extrovert kind.' In 1950, Yale's president, Alfred Whitney Griswold, reassured alumni that the Yale man of the future would not be a 'beetle-browed, highly specialized intellectual, but a well-rounded man.' It wasn't until the 1950s that these sort of barriers were dropped against Jewish Americans and their numbers started to rise again at elite universities."*

The above section isn't meant to imply that Asians are the "new Jews." It's meant to show the potential consequences of "black box" admissions criteria and how disgusting those practices can be. Opaque processes can be subject to considerable abuse.

Why This Matters

The elite schools of America hold considerable power. For much of this nation's history, they've been the gatekeepers of wealth, prestige, and knowledge. Entry into their club confers privilege — it's a signal to the world that you are among the chosen to be selected for high paying jobs, leadership positions, and power.

In today's world, it seems hard to fathom that federally-funded, tax-exempt institutions could continue to shroud their selection criteria in secrecy. It's likely that admissions officers are wonderful people, but what if every time they see an Asian applicant, they subconsciously think: "Another piano playing, hard working kid, with perfect SAT scores. Good candidate, but we can't have a campus entirely full of people like that." Is that an okay thought today? Does it lead to outcomes that represent our societal values? Will it be okay to think that way in 20 years?

The nature of what is "merit" is constructed by those who control the admissions decisions. Before the early 20th century, it was how good you were at Latin and Greek. Later, what kind of family you came from become important. Today, the holistic admissions criteria are a black box.

Many Asians believe they are being held to a different academic standard than whites. This belief might be true or false, but universities should release the data that puts the debate to rest. But if Asians are underrepresented on American college campuses relative to what their academic performance would predict, this seems like the sort of discrimination that history would ultimately judge very harshly.

9.

THE FOOD INDUSTRIAL COMPLEX

In 2011, during a debate over the nutritional guidelines for school lunches, Congress decided that pizza counted as a vegetable. And not for the first time.

The U.S. government first proposed that an unhealthy food, if it contains trace amounts of a healthy ingredient, could count as a vegetable, in 1981. Looking for ways to cut the school lunch budget, the Reagan Administration suggested that cafeterias could count ingredients in condiments like pickle relish and ketchup toward nutritional requirements.

This was not good politics. The press and Democratic opposition had a field day saying that Reagan had just classified ketchup as a vegetable. "This is one of the most ridiculous regulations I ever heard of," Senator John Heinz, owner of Heinz ketchup, told the press, "and I suppose I need not add that I know something about ketchup and relish."

The Reagan Administration dropped the proposal, but it soon became law anyway. When the Obama Administration directed the U.S. Department of Agriculture to revise school lunch policies, experts took aim at the rule that allowed the tiny amount of tomato paste in pizza sauce to count toward the vegetable requirements of each meal.

Any changes could jeopardize huge contracts for companies that supply food for school children's lunches, so the food industry spent some $5.6 million lobbying Congress to protect its interests. According to Margo Wootan, director of the Center for Science in the Public Interest, two multibillion dollar companies spent the most: Schwan and ConAgra, which each had large contracts for pizzas and fries used in school lunches.

Before the U.S. Department of Agriculture (USDA) could even make its recommendations, Congress acted to make sure the push for healthier lunches did not hurt the manufacturers of unhealthy foods. Congress passed an agriculture appropriations bill that would deny the USDA funding to enforce any policies that prevented the potatoes in french fries or the tomato paste in pizza from counting as nutritional elements.

The press enjoyed declaring that Congress had classified pizza as a vegetable. Cynics shrugged at yet another example of the government prioritizing the bottom line of businesses that manufacture sugary and salty processed foods over public health.

Yet the one-sided nature of the food industry's lobbying is puzzling. Where were the broccoli, spinach, and carrot lobbies? Why didn't a member of Congress take to the floor with a set of talking points provided by the leafy green vegetable lobby? Why can't American farmers, who enjoy huge government subsidies, stand up to the processed food lobby?

The answer lies in the economics of the food industry. The possibility of branding processed foods — like Fruit Loops cereal, Chips Ahoy cookies, and Ritz crackers — and selling them at high markups means that the market for processed foods dwarfs the much less lucrative business of farming fruits and vegetables. Those high markups also provide ample funding to buy access to Congress, the White House, and organizations like the USDA that set nutrition policy.

In addition, while large commercial farms do enjoy substantial access to policy makers in Washington, "Big Ag" is not in the healthy food business. American farms with lobbying power don't grow brussel sprouts; they grow grains used to make the high fructose corn syrup in Coke, the starches in processed foods, and the oil in deep fryers. This is somewhat inevitable — a reflection of fruits' and vegetables' limited role in the world food economy. But it is also a self-inflicted wound on American (and global) health — the result of misguided government policy that subsidizes the production of foods and beverages like Big Macs and Big Gulps.

The Poor Margins of Broccoli Farmers

In Washington, "the food lobby" has become synonymous with unhealthy food. In 2013, according to the Center for Responsive Politics, processed food manufacturers spent $40 million lobbying while the fruit and vegetable industry spent a mere $4.8 million. Moreover, two of the top three fruit and vegetable contributors were a company that grows tomatoes for fast food chains and the National Potato Council, which protects potato farmers interests in french fries.

To understand why the food lobby is dominated by companies pushing unhealthy foods, a good place to start is the huge imbalance between the amount of fruits and vegetables we should eat and the relative size of the fruits and vegetables market.

According to nutritional guidelines published by the USDA and the Harvard School of Public Health, fruits and vegetables should make up about 50% of a healthy diet. But the financial value of the fruit and vegetable market is nowhere near 50% of the food industry. In

2012, the USDA calculated that American farms earned $47 billion in revenue from fruits, vegetables, and nuts. In contrast, just three American processed food manufacturers had (global) revenues of $116.2 billion in 2013.

The meat and carb heavy American diet partially explains these disparities. The Department of Agriculture estimates that Americans eat roughly 50% less fruits and vegetables and over 20% more grains and meat than recommended by its nutrition guidelines.

But it is the economics of the food industry that really explain why the food lobby is an unhealthy one. Processed foods have high margins that fund large advertising campaigns, support substantial lobbying budgets, and increase the size of the market; the importance of branding also leads to consolidation that supports special interest lobbying. In contrast, farmers growing fruits and vegetables make a commodity with low markups. There is little money for lobbying and advertising, a smaller market, and fewer mega-companies with big bullhorns in Washington.

To see these dynamics in action, let's compare the economics of selling vegetables with a processed food like cereal.

When John Harvey Kellogg and Charles Post began selling the first modern cereals in the 19th century, they tried to protect their cereal making techniques using patents and lawsuits. They failed. Their product was simply processed wheat or corn, and its production was easy to replicate.

Despite today's variation, which derive mostly from different shapes and added flavors, cereal is at its core a cheap, nearly identical product. So cereal companies turned to advertising and branding to protect their share of the market. In Eat Your Heart Out, Felicity Lawrence writes that as Charles Post began selling Grape Nuts, he declared that "The sunshine that makes a business plant grow is advertising" and marketed his cereal as "brain food" that could cure not only malaria but also diseases of his own invention. The Quaker symbol of Quaker Oats became the first nationally recognized cereal brand; cereals marketed under the name Kellogg's followed. And, of course, as cereal manufacturers battled for control of the rapidly expanding market, they added hefty doses of sugar to make their "horse food" more palatable.

The importance of branding and marketing doesn't lend itself to a decentralized market of small cereal makers; it means huge corporations with high margins. In 2013, Kellogg's reported that of every $1 consumers spent on its cereal, it earned 41 cents of gross profit; the company is currently worth $24.1 billion.

Kellogg's has a $24 billion market capitalization and trades on the New York Stock Exchange because it does not just make cereal. It also owns Pringles and manufactures a variety of processed foods from Eggo Waffles to Famous Amos chocolate chip cookies. The entire processed foods industry is similarly consolidated; if you follow your favorite snack food up the food chain, you'll usually find that it is owned by a gigantic multinational company. PepsiCo owns Funyuns, Rold Gold pretzels, and Sun Chips. Ritz crackers, Oreos, and Wheat Thins sell under the Nabisco label, which is owned by Mondelēz International. So whenever a federal agency or Congress makes a push to support healthy foods, it essentially picks a fight with a collection of the world's largest companies.

It is possible to market fruits and vegetables and sell them at a markup. Honeycrisp apples, designed for that satisfying crunch when you bite into one, enjoys a high price premium two to three times other varieties. "Organic" has emerged as a powerful marketing tool, and prices of kale increased 25% over the past 3 years. Distributors use tactics like selling produce in convenient sizes (such as one snack's worth of baby carrots) to differentiate their products.

In general, though, consumers treat fruits and vegetables as identical commodities. The honeycrisp apple is a rarity, and trends like kale-mania benefit the market rather than a single company. Companies do market veggies, but as Dr. Roberta Cook of UC Davis's agriculture program notes, brand recognition is low. Brands need a year round presence on supermarket shelves so consumers can recognize the brand and purchase it routinely, but produce is generally seasonal. Efforts to link recognized brands with a certain quality level and a higher price point is hindered by the influence of weather on produce quality and prices.

Farmers and companies involved in produce distribution simply provide a commodity at the going price, and the result is a much smaller, leaner, and less centralized industry than the processed food industry. Although fruits and vegetables are seen as high value crops, the majority of small to medium sized farms are actually not profitable; those farmers support themselves with non-farm incomes. Even the USDA's most optimistic estimates of the profit margins of large commercial vegetable farms are half those of processed foods like cereal — the cost of growing produce eats up most of the profits. The top 9% of vegetable farms, according to a 2007 agriculture census, have annual sales over $500,000. That's substantial, but it hardly compares to PepsiCo's revenues.

The term processed foods also applies to more than just Oreos and Doritos. When we think of pasta sauce, we normally don't think of junk food. But as Michael Moss writes in the New York Times Magazine, products like Preggo pasta sauce contain huge amounts of salt and sugar, just like potato chips and cereal. The processed food industry, then, is profitable, politically powerful, and even more enormous than we realize. Is it any surprise that the food lobby is synonymous with unhealthy foods?

An Exercise in Mislabeling

The power of the food lobby to protect processed foods from antagonistic policies can be seen in its response to the 1990 Nutrition Labeling and Education Act. Before 1990, food labels that listed ingredients and nutritional content were optional and opposed by food manufacturers. The act, based on recommendations from the Food and Drug Administration, sought to make it mandatory for the first time.

An article in the New York Times in the early 1990s highlights some of the processed food industry's subversion tactics. Spokesmen claimed that the labeling requirement would cost billions of dollars to implement and put out studies that purported to show that consumers preferred extremely uninformative labels. Above all, lobbyists stressed that the labels would be too confusing for consumers. "If you are not [the Commissioner of the FDA], who has a law degree and medical degrees," Jeffrey Nedelman, a vice president of the Grocery Manufacturers Association, told the paper, "you are not going to be able to make sense out of all this information. The labels need to be consumer friendly."

The legislation did pass — a reminder that not all attempts to legislate health are doomed. But food lobbyists also managed to carve out exemptions and even loopholes that could assist processed foods' marketing strategies. Kraft Cheese, for example, went to the White House to make sure it could keep marketing its cheese as low fat; the first Bush Administration accepted the new rules only after the FDA raised the maximum fat content for low fat foods.

The most prominent loophole, which nutrition expert Marion Nestle describes in Food Politics, was that food manufacturers could market products with the word "healthy" with very few restrictions. Similarly, the legislation allowed companies to market the benefits of a product based on a single, minor ingredient. It is this loophole that allows Kellogg's to add vitamin D to its cereal and then market its super sugary Frosted Flakes as "a good source of vitamin D." This is also the reason that the boxes of so many sugar-laden cereals describe them as "part of a healthy breakfast."

The Nutrition Labeling and Education Act became law, but it also demonstrates how food lobbyists oppose public-minded legislation and can even shape it in its favor.

The McDonaldization of the American Farm

American farmers receive billions of dollars in subsidies every year, which they lobby fiercely to protect. In the first 3 months of 2012, as lawmakers began debating farm subsidies as part of an extension of the U.S. farm bill, the American Farm Bureau spent $6 million pressuring Congress. So why aren't American farmers as successful in pushing legislation that favors fresh produce and "real food" as they are at winning subsidies?

The answer lies in recognizing that the prototypical American farm does not produce healthy food. Companies like Whole Foods promote organic food with images of idyllic farms, but farms with a variety of crops and livestock are not representative of American agriculture. As food journalist Michael Pollan has written in the New York Times Magazine, America's large commercial farms are monocultures, meaning they specialize in a single crop, which is usually a grain. Together, corn and soy account for almost 50% of all American crop revenues.

According to Rosamond Naylor and Walter Falcon of Stanford University, America's corn crop is used to produce half of the sweeteners Americans consume every year in beer and soda. The majority of the crop goes toward feeding cattle (46%) and ethanol production (25%). Corn also provides the starchy base for processed foods and the oil for McDonald's deep fryers. The portion of crops from large commercial farms that does directly feed people essentially makes our least healthy foods.

The dominance of grains in American agriculture is not unusual. Just four grains — corn, wheat, rice, and soy — account for so much of global agricultural output that economists modeling food prices only look at the market for these grains. Naylor and Falcon note that countries' agriculture policy (including that of the United States) has been to increase the yields of these grains. After all, higher yields intuitively mean more productive farms, wealthier farmers, more food, and less hunger.

These policies are substantial enough that American agriculture does not experience a free market. (Nor do farmers anywhere in the world.) The origins of modern intervention in agriculture were sown during the Great Depression, when a glut of crops and weak demand led to decreasing prices and dire circumstances for American farmers. In response, the U.S. government propped up prices by paying farmers to leave farmland barren and buying surplus crops to destroy or ship overseas as food aid. Further legislation cemented the government's role in subsidizing prices, often by buying grains directly at inflated prices. Today the government no longer pays farmers not to grow crops, but it provides subsidies by paying insurance premiums.

Each piece of legislation responded to low crop prices and the perception that the market insufficiently rewarded farmers. At the same time, as related by

Michael Pollan, the concentration of American agriculture into large monocultures was no accident, but the result of American policy choices. The government promoted the research and production of chemical fertilizers, pesticides, and higher yield grains; the Department of Agriculture also encouraged farms to "get big or get out." The government did not dole out the decades of generous subsidies described above indiscriminately; subsidies went specifically to subsidize the production of corn, soybeans, wheat, and rice at a large scale.

In some ways, these policies have been a great success. American farms are profitable — a 2007 report on the farm bill found that 10% of America's farms, which produce 75% of its agricultural yield, make $200,000 in income — and extremely productive — Pollan points out that the average corn belt farmer now feeds around 140 people. In addition, the average American now enjoys half a pound of meat per day — an amount once considered princely.

In contemporary America, however, where the majority of Americans get too many calories rather than too few, these policies no longer make any sense. In its push for large monocultures, and in order to buy the peace of specialized vegetable farms, the USDA prohibited farms that received grain subsidies from growing fruits and vegetables. This put the American government in the insane position of subsidizing the cost of fast food while actively prohibiting some farms from growing fruits and vegetables.

Even farm animals, which are cheaper to raise when they can be fed with subsidized grain, have a mixed nutrition record. Most nutritionists consider meat part of a healthy diet, but they also believe Americans eat too much meat. In addition, grain subsidies, as well as the lack of any policy prohibiting the regular use of antibiotics in animal feed, enable farmers to raise animals at scale in confined areas. (The antibiotics keep animals alive in the filthy conditions of small cages.) This author does not want to pay more for steak, but it is this system that makes McDonald's hamburgers and Kentucky Fried Chicken cheaper than healthier foods.

America's large, profitable farms spend millions on lobbying each year and enjoy substantial access to lawmakers. The problem is that almost none of these farms provide a counterweight to manufacturers of junk and processed foods. Farms' lobbying power protects french fries, Big Macs, and soda rather than leafy greens. It's the nature of the grain-dominated world food economy, but it's also a market that is supported by bad agriculture policy that pushes farms to grow crops for unhealthy foods.

The Food Pyramid's Corrupt Foundation

With this understanding of America's food industry, we can understand a certain mystery behind the food pyramid.

In 1992, the United States Department of Agriculture unveiled the food pyramid, its guide to healthy eating. Thanks to government efforts to publicize it — pushing it into doctors' offices and home economics classes — the majority of Americans recognize the food pyramid. As the nutritional guidelines behind the food pyramid also inform policy like school lunches and food stamps, the food pyramid is likely the most influential nutrition document in the country's history.

In its twenty-two year lifespan, however, the food pyramid has seen a surprising amount of change. The base of the original pyramid contained loaves of bread, plates of pasta, and bowls of cereal; the next layer had fruits and vegetables; the next dairy, meat, and other protein-rich foods. The advice seemed clear: a healthy diet includes plenty of grains that are rich in carbohydrates, as well as fruits and vegetables.

The USDA replaced the pyramid with a revised food plate in 2011. In the new plate, grains no longer dominate. Grains and vegetables each represent 30% of the plate; fruit and protein each take up another 20%. The changes do not represent a new understanding of nutrition; the story of the food pyramid is just the most highly visible demonstration of the food and agriculture sectors' lobbying prowess.

Dr. Luise Light is a nutrition expert and led the team at the Department of Agriculture that made the original recommendations for the food pyramid. If you review her original recommendations, they sounds very similar to dietary advice given by nutritionists today: lots of vegetables, more lean sources of protein like fish and nuts, and less dairy and processed foods.

Those guidelines, according to Dr. Light, did not survive their trip to the office of the Head of the Department of Agriculture. In a 2004 account, she described herself as "shocked" by the changes that were made. Her team placed fruits and vegetables at the base of the pyramid and whole-grain breads and cereals further up. The new guidelines not only switched carbohydrates to the base of the pyramid, it moved processed foods like crackers and corn flakes, which Dr. Light and her team had placed at the top of the pyramid with chocolate, to the base of the pyramid. Even with all the edits, the food pyramid was not released for another 12 years.

With an understanding of the food lobby, it's not hard to understand why. The multinational companies that make processed foods and large American farms that produce starchy products wanted to see carb-heavy foods promoted at the base of the pyramid; the tiny leafy greens lobby was too tiny to make its voice heard. As in 1992, every five years, when the Department of Agriculture revisits its nutrition guidelines, the food industry gears up by releasing floods of reports, nominating researchers that sit on industry boards to be part of the USDA committee reviewing the policies, and appealing to allies in Congress and the White House. This means that new policies are always a battle between public-interest organizations pushing for healthier guidelines and industry that is almost universally working to subvert them.

An Unhealthy Lobby

The American government wields enormous influence over our diet. Federal policy shapes a farm system that could not be farther from a free market and influences what millions of schoolchildren eat every day at lunch. As long as food lobbyists overwhelmingly represent the makers of unhealthy food, health advocates will always struggle to push policy in a healthier direction.

To some extent, this is inevitable. The profit margins for making a well branded bar of sugar are better than for growing brussel sprouts, which creates more money for lobbying against labeling laws, sugar taxes, and so on. But the current status quo, in which American farms grow crops for unhealthy products like high fructose corn syrup, is the result of misinformed agricultural policy. The latest farm bill, passed in 2014, reduced some of the most egregious farm subsidies and provided funding to support fruit and vegetable farming. Policy that ceased skewing American agriculture in an unhealthy direction entirely would make the voice of American farmers a healthier one.

"Good advice about nutrition conflicts with the interests of many big industries," Michael Jacobson, cofounder of the Center for Science in the Public Interest, once said, "each of which has more lobbying power than all the public-interest groups combined." But the real problem is that within industry, manufacturers of unhealthy food are so much more powerful than the makers of health food that the food lobby has become synonymous with the foods driving our obesity epidemic.

10.

WHY IS SCIENCE BEHIND
A PAYWALL?

Scientists' work follows a consistent pattern. They apply for grants, perform their research, and publish the results in a journal. The process is so routine that it almost seems inevitable. But what if it's not the best way to do science?

Although the act of publishing seems to entail sharing research with the world, most published papers sit behind paywalls. The journals that publish them charge thousands of dollars per subscription, putting access out of reach to all but the most minted universities. Subscription costs have risen dramatically over the past generation. According to critics, those increases are the result of the consolidation of journals by private companies that unduly profit off their market share of scientific knowledge.

Investigating these alleged scrooges of the science world, we discovered that their opponents believe that the battle against this parasitic profiting is only one part of the scientific process that needs to be fixed.

Advocates of "open science" argue that the current model of science, developed in the 1600s, needs to change and take full advantage of the Internet to share research and collaborate in the discovery making process. When the entire scientific community can connect instantly online, they argue, there is simply no reason for research teams to work in silos and share their findings according to the publishing schedules of journals.

Subscriptions limit access to scientific knowledge. And when careers are made and tenures earned by publishing in prestigious journals, then sharing datasets, collaborating with other scientists, and crowdsourcing difficult problems are disincentivized. Following 17th century practices, open science advocates insist, limits the progress of science in the 21st.

The Creation of Academic Journals

*"If I have seen further it is by standing on
the shoulders of giants."*
(Isaac Newton)

In the 17th century, scientists often kept their discoveries secret. Isaac Newton and Gottfried Leibniz argued over which of them first invented calculus because Isaac Newton did not publish his invention for decades. Robert Hooke, Leonardo da Vinci, and Galileo Galilei published encoded messages proving their discoveries. Scientists gained little by sharing their research other than claiming their spot in history. As a result, many chose to keep their discoveries secret and build off their findings, only revealing how to decode their message when the next man or woman made the same discovery.

Public funding of research and its distribution in scholarly journals began at this time. Wealthy patrons pooled their money to create scientific academies like England's Royal Society and the French Academy of

Sciences, allowing scientists to pursue their research in a stable, funded environment. By subsidizing research, they hoped to aid its creation and dissemination for society's benefit.

Academic journals developed in the 1660s as an efficient way for the new academies to spread their findings. The first started when Henry Oldenburg, secretary of the Royal Society, published the society's articles at his own expense. At the time, the market for scientific articles was small and publishing a major expense. Scientists gave away the articles for free because the publisher provided a great value in spreading the findings at very little profit. When the journals market became more formal, almost all publishers were non-profits, often associated with research institutions. Up until the mid 20th century, profits were low and private publishers were rare.

Universities have since replaced academies as the dominant scientific institution. Due to the rising costs of research (think linear accelerators), governments replaced individual patrons as the biggest subsidizers of science, with researchers applying for grants from the government or foundations to fund research projects. And journals transitioned from a means to publish findings to take on the role of a marker of prestige. Scientists' most important qualification today is their publication history.

Many contemporary researchers work in the private sector, where the profit incentives of intellectual property incentivize scientific discovery. But outside of research with immediate commercial applications, the system developed in the 1600s has remained a relative constant. As physicist turned science writer Michael Nielsen notes, this system facilitated "a scientific culture which to this day rewards the sharing of discoveries with jobs and prestige for the discoverer... It has changed surprisingly little in the last 300 years."

The Monopolization of Science

In April 2012, the Harvard Library published a letter stating that its subscriptions to academic journals were "financially untenable." Due to price increases as high as 145% over the past 6 years, the library said that it would soon be forced to cut back on subscriptions. The Harvard Library singled out one group as primarily responsible for the problem: "This situation is exacerbated by efforts of certain publishers (called "providers") to acquire, bundle, and increase the pricing on journals."

The most famous of these providers is Elsevier. It is a behemoth. Every year it publishes 250,000 articles in 2,000 journals. Its 2012 revenues reached $2.7 billion, and Elsevier's profits of over $1 billion account for 45% of the Reed Elsevier Group — its parent company which is the 495th largest company in the world in terms of market capitalization.

Companies like Elsevier developed in the 1960s and 1970s. They bought academic journals from the non-profits and academic societies that ran them, successfully betting that they could raise prices without losing customers. Today just three publishers, Elsevier, Springer and Wiley, account for roughly 42% of all articles published in the over $19 billion academic publishing market for science, technology, engineering, and medical research. University libraries account for 80% of their customers.

Since every article is published in only one journal and researchers ideally want access to every article in their field, libraries buy subscriptions no matter the price. From 1984 to 2002, for example, the price of science journals increased nearly 600%. One estimate puts Elsevier's prices at 642% higher than industry-wide averages.

These providers also bundle journals together. Critics argue that this forces libraries to buy less prestigious journals to gain access to indispensable offerings. There is no set cost for a bundle; instead providers like Elsevier structure plans in response to each institution's past history of subscriptions.

The tactics of Elsevier and its ilk have made them an evil empire in the eyes of their critics — the science professors, library administrators, PhD students, independent researchers, science companies, and interested individuals who find their efforts to access information thwarted by Elsevier's paywalls. They cite two main objections.

The first is that prices are increasing at a time when the Internet has made it cheaper and easier than ever before to share information. The second is that universities are paying for research that they themselves produced. Universities fund research with grants and pay the salaries of the researchers behind every paper. Even peer review, which Elsevier cites as a major value it adds by checking the validity of papers and publishing only significant and valuable findings, is performed on a volunteer basis by professors on university salaries.

Elsevier actively responds to each challenge to its legitimacy and speaks of "work[ing] in partnership with the research community to make real and sustainable contributions to science." Deutsche Bank, in an investor analyst report, summarizes Elsevier's arguments:

> *"In justifying the margins earned, the publishers point to the highly skilled nature of the staff they employ (to pre-vet submitted papers prior to the peer review process), the support they provide to the peer review panels, including modest*

*stipends, the complex typesetting, printing
and distribution activities, including Web
publishing and hosting. REL [Reed
Elsevier] employs around 7,000 people in
its Science business as a whole. REL also
argues that the high margins reflect
economies of scale and the very high levels
of efficiency with which they operate."*

One way to test the validity of Elsevier's defense is to compare the cost of for-profit and non-profit journals. Within ecology, for example, the price per page of a for-profit journal is nearly three times that of a non-profit. When comparing on the basis of the price per citation (an indicator of a paper's quality and influence), non-profit papers do more than five times better. Another method is to examine Elsevier's profit margins, which at 36% are well above the average of 4%-5% for the periodical publishing business. Given that Elsevier performs a centuries old practice, it's hard to perceive its high margins as reflective of anything other than charging extortionate rates for a product (scientific articles) with no substitute. The aforementioned Deutsche Bank report concludes similarly:

*"We believe the [Elsevier] adds relatively
little value to the publishing process. We
are not attempting to dismiss what 7,000
people at [Elsevier] do for a living. We are
simply observing that if the process really
were as complex, costly and value-added
as the publishers protest that it is, 40%
margins wouldn't be available."*

The high cost of journal subscriptions has been recognized as a problem at least as far back as reporting done by The Economist in 1998. But now even the world's wealthiest university cannot afford to purchase access to new scientific knowledge — even though universities fund and perform that research.

No One to Blame but Ourselves

For critics of private publishers' monopolization of the journal industry, there is a simple solution: open access journals. Like traditional journals, they accept submissions, manage a peer review process, and publish articles. But they charge no subscription fees and make all their articles available free online. To cover costs, open access journals instead charge researchers publication fees around $2,000. (Reviewers who are not on payroll decide which papers to accept in order to spare journals the temptation of accepting every paper and raking in the dough.) Unlike traditional journals, which claim exclusive copyright to the papers they publish, open access (OA) journals are free of almost all copyright restrictions.

If universities source the funding for research, and its researchers perform both the research and peer review, why don't they all switch to OA journals? There have been some notable successes in the form of the Public Library of Science's well-regarded open access journals. However, current scientific culture makes it hard to switch.

A history of publication in prestigious journals is a prerequisite to every step on the career ladder of a scientist. Every paper submitted to a new, unproven OA journal is one that could have been published in heavyweights like Science or Nature. And even if a tenured or idealistic professor is willing to make that sacrifice, what about their PhD students and co-authors for whom publication in a prestigious journal could mean everything?

Governments could push science toward an open access future by mandating that publicly financed research be made publicly available. Every year, the United States government provides over $60 billion in public grants for scientific research. In 2008, Congress mandated (over furious opposition from private publishers) that all research funded through the National Institute of Health, which accounts for 50% of government funding of science, be made publicly available within a year. Extending this requirement to all other research financed by the government would go a long way for OA publishing. This is true of similar efforts by the British and Canadian governments, which are in the midst of such steps.

The Costs of Closed Publishing: The Reinhart-Rogoff Paper

The controversy over the 2010 paper *"Growth In A Time of Debt,"* published by Harvard economists Carmen Reinhart and Kenneth Rogoff in the American Economic Review, illustrates some of the problems with the journal system.

The paper used a dataset of countries' GDP growth and debt levels to suggest that countries with public debts over 90% of their GDP grow significantly slower than countries with more modest levels of debt.

To the media that covered their findings and the politicians and technocrats that cited it, the message was clear: debt is bad and austerity (reducing government spending) is good. Although they discussed their findings with more nuance, Reinhart and Rogoff obliged Washington by discussing how their findings supported the case for deficit reduction.

But this past April, a group of researchers from UMass Amherst revealed a flaw in the Reinhart-Rogoff paper. Like many economists, the researchers had been trying unsuccessfully to replicate Reinhart and Rogoff's findings. Only when the Harvard economists shared their original dataset and Excel spreadsheet did the UMass team discover why no one could replicate the findings: the economists had made an Excel error.

Reinhart and Rogoff forgot to include 5 cells of data. Noting this mistake, and the exclusion of a number of years of high debt growth in several countries and a weighting system that they found questionable, the UMass team declared that the effect disappeared. Instead of contracting 0.1%, the average growth rate of countries with debt over 90% of GDP was a respectable 2.2%. The mistake was caught, but for 2 years the false finding influenced policy-makers and informed the work of other economists.

Bad Incentives

Moving to open access journals would expand access to scientific knowledge, but if it preserves the idolization of the research paper, then the work of science reformers is incomplete.

Reformers argue that the current journal system slows down the publication of science research. Peer review rarely takes less than a month, and journals often ask for papers to be rewritten or new analyses undertaken, which stretches out publication for half a year or more. While quality control is necessary, thanks to the Internet, articles don't need to be in a final form before they are shared. Michael Eisen, co-founder of the Public Library of Science, also notes that, in his experience, "the most important technical flaws are uncovered after papers are published."

People celebrate the discovery of new drugs, theories, and social phenomena. But if we conceptualize science as crossing out a list of possible hypotheses to improve our odds of hitting on the correct one, then experiments that fail are just as important to publish as successful ones.

Journals could not remain prestigious, however, if they published litanies of failed experiments. As a result, the scientific community lacks an efficient way to learn about disproven hypotheses. Worse, it encourages researchers to cherry pick their data and express full confidence in a conclusion that the data and their gut may not fully support. Until science moves beyond the journal system, we may never know how many false positives are produced by this type of fraud-light.

A Scientific Process for the 21st Century

Although scientists are the cutting edge, there are many examples of missed opportunities to make the scientific process more efficient through technology.

In our conversation with Banyan, a startup whose core mission is open science, CEO Toni Gemayel revealed just how much low hanging fruit is out there. "We want to go after peer review," he says. "Lots of people still print their papers and [physically] give them to professors for review or put them in Word documents that have no software compatibility." Banyan recently launched a public beta version of its product — tools that allow researchers to share, collaborate on, and publish research. "The basis of the company," Gemayel explains, "is that scientists will go open source if given simple, beneficial tools."

Physicist turned open science advocate Michael Nielsen is an eloquent voice on what new tools could facilitate an open culture of sharing and collaboration. One existing tool that he advocates is arXiv, which allows physicists to share "preprints" of early drafts. This facilitates feedback on ongoing work and disseminates findings faster. Another practice he advocates — publishing all data and source code used in research projects alongside papers — has long been endorsed by scientists and could be accomplished within the journal framework.

In his essay "The Future of Science," Nielsen also imagines new tools that don't yet exist. A system of wikis, for example, that allow scientists to maintain perfectly up to date "super-textbooks" on their field for reference by fellow researchers. Or an efficient system for scientists to benefit from the expertise of scientists in other fields when their research "gives rise to problems in areas" in which they are not experts. After all, even Einstein needed help from mathematicians working on new forms of geometry to build his General Theory of Relativity.

But none of these ideas are likely to take off on a mass scale until scientists have clear incentives to contribute to them. Since publication history is all too often the sole metric by which a scientist's work is judged, researchers who primarily assemble data sets for others to use or maintain a public wiki of meta-knowledge will not progress in their careers.

Addressing this issue, Gemayel references the open spirit amongst coders working on open-source software. "There's no reward system right now for open science," he says. "Scientists' careers don't benefit from it. But in software, everyone wants to see your GitHub account." Talented coders who could make good money freelancing often pour hours of unpaid work into open-source software, which is free to use and adapt for any purpose.

On one hand, many people do so to work on interesting problems and as part of an ethos of contributing to its development. Thousands of companies and services would simply not exist without the development of open-source software. But coders also benefit personally from open-source work because the rest of the field recognizes its value. Employers look at applicants' open-source work via their GitHub accounts (by publicly showing their software work, GitHub accounts can effectively function as a resume), and people generally respect the contributions people make via open-source projects and sharing valuable tips in blog posts and comments. It's the type of open pursuit that you would expect in science. But we see it more in Silicon Valley because it is valued and benefits people's careers.

Disrupting Science

"The process of scientific discovery – how we do science – will change more over the next 20 years than in the past 300 years."
(Michael Nielsen)

The current model of publicly funding research and publishing it in academic journals was developed during the days of Isaac Newton in response to 17th century problems.

Beginning in the 1960s, private companies began to buy up and profit off the copyrights they enjoyed as the publishers of new scientific knowledge. This has caused a panic among cash-strapped university libraries. But the bigger problem may be that scientists have not fully utilized the Internet to share, collaborate, and invent new ways of doing science. The impact of this failure is "impossible to measure or put an upper bound on," Gemayel tells us. "We don't know what could have been created or solved if knowledge wasn't paywalled. What if Tim Berners-Lee had put the world wide web behind a paywall. Or patented it?"

Advocates of open science present a strong case that the idolization of publishing articles in journals has resulted in too much secrecy, too many false positives, and a reduction in the rate at which scientific discoveries are made. Only by changing the culture and incentives among scientists can a system of openness and collaboration be fostered. The Internet was created to help scientists share their research. It seems overdue that scientists take full advantage of its original purpose.

11.

IS COLLEGE WORTH IT?

American colleges and universities are enduring a crisis of faith among the public. Although a college degree has long been heralded as a ticket to the middle or upper class, the cost of college has increased faster than the price of health care, housing, or just about anything else over the past 30 years. Tuitions, student debt, and student loan default rates have all skyrocketed, leading indebted graduates to malign their degrees and pundits to argue that college is not worth the price tag.

Despite the pessimism, research on the financial value of a college degree all concurs: A bachelor's degree is a sound and increasingly valuable investment. The extra income graduates earn more than compensates for the high cost.

College should not necessarily be justified strictly by its financial payoff. But appeals to the value of a liberal arts education or cultivating civic virtue and lifelong friendships are moot for all but a wealthy minority if a college education is prohibitively expensive.

How do we resolve this paradox that college is a sound financial investment, yet an increasing number of students find themselves unable to pay back their loans? When it comes to educating students and preparing them for careers without indebting them, how do we grade American higher education?

College may still, on average, be a worthwhile investment. But for American colleges and universities, a 'D' is still a passing grade.

The Supersizing of American Colleges

Over the past three decades, American colleges and universities have been supersized. More students are paying higher tuitions — financed by more financial aid and more debt — to attend colleges with expanding budgets that fund more programs and more facilities.

Historic tuition prices offer a stark reminder of escalating costs. If tuitions and fees had only increased at the rate of inflation since 1987, today's smartphone toting Millennials would pay $25,268 to attend Yale instead of $42,300. Amherst College students would pay $24,741 instead of $44,610. Michigan residents would pay $5,815 at the University of Michigan instead of $13,819.

Despite skyrocketing tuitions, many college administrators can still look parents in the eye and say that college is not crazy expensive. Adjusted for inflation, the amount of financial aid provided by the federal government in the form of grants and loans increased from $12.5 billion in 1982 to nearly $170 billion today, and selective colleges offer enough grant money that only a minority of wealthy families pay full sticker price. Between 1995 and 2007, net prices, or the price students paid after accounting for financial aid, increased 20% at four year public schools (compared to a 56% increase in full tuition) and 27% at four year private schools (compared to a 39% increase in full tuition). That's a more modest increase, but still substantial for an already expensive service.

One of America's greatest concerns is that college now pushes too many students to take on an unsustainable amount of debt. Outstanding student debt stands at $1 trillion, the result of an explosion of debt over the past 10 years. Surveys of former students by the Federal Reserve Bank of New York show that average debt per student increased from under $15,000 in 2004 to $25,000 today, while the percentage of students defaulting on their loans increased from 9.5% to over 17%. While it could be comforting to simply blame the explosion of debt and delinquency on the recession, the upward trends began before the economy imploded.

So why has college become so expensive?

Experts debate a number of potential reasons. Cutting edge research centers have become increasingly expensive. (Think linear accelerators instead of microscopes.) Colleges also compete for professors and administrators in a labor market of well-educated professionals that is increasingly productive and well-compensated, which drives up salary costs.

But a primary reason — and in our opinion, a very convincing one — is that colleges have no reason not to spend more and raise tuition prices. After all, few people shop for "bargains" in higher education; an expensive price tag typically indicates prestige. That leaves one clear strategy for a school seeking higher standing: fundraise, increase tuition, and spend, spend, spend.

Each year, schools compete for a limited pool of talented students who — especially at the most selective schools — are fairly insensitive to price. What's another $2,000 a year for your daughter's future and the best four years of her life? This leads to a spending race to woo wealthy, accomplished students with big name faculty and fancy buildings. Since all that matters is a university's prestige relative to its peers, everyone needs to constantly raise funds and spend to outpace other schools.

At some point, colleges should hit a wall when not enough students can afford the high price tag — especially at non-Ivy schools. But since the government wants education to be affordable, the amount of aid available has increased in step with tuitions. As subsidies increase, colleges can afford to raise tuition and spend money on more programs, buildings, and administrator salaries, effectively capturing the subsidy.

As a result, the default over the past decades has been spending more to get more, not doing more with less. Last year, the president of Ohio State University told the New York Times, "I didn't think a lot about costs. I do not think we have given significant thought to the impact of college costs on families."

Worse, students may be paying more for an education that delivers less and less core value. In their book Academically Adrift, two sociologists find that class and study time at colleges has dwindled well below 40 hours a week and that 36% of students gain no critical thinking skills during college.

All these fact suggest a simple narrative: Colleges have used more and more easy money to build nicer buildings, launch new programs, and pay administrators higher salaries, to the point that the cost of college has outweighed the returns. The perception of college as a golden ticket is a mirage; the reality is underemployed graduates mired in debt. But is this narrative true?

The Case for College

With so many graduates struggling with debt, intuitively it seems that a number of schools must churn out graduates who don't earn enough to cover the cost of their education. Yet looking at data and research on the prospects of college graduates is unambiguous: College is a sound financial investment that offers excellent returns.

Every year, a company called Payscale draws on its national data set of employee salaries and educational backgrounds to rank colleges by their "return on investment." Its analysis asks one question: given the cost of a school's tuition, fees, and living expenses, as well as the amount of money one could make in the workforce without attending college, how much more money do students make by attending a particular college? Payscale answers the question by using real data on the salary earned by graduates of each school over a thirty year career.

The analysis reveals some interesting patterns. Engineering schools offer the greatest financial payoff. Ivy League schools have the highest tuitions but also the greatest financial returns of any non-engineering college. In general, a degree from a research university is a better investment than one from a smaller college. And many public schools perform well in the analysis, allowing graduates to reap the same financial rewards as graduates of pricier, private schools.

Most importantly, Payscale's analysis finds that college is a very sound investment. Over a 30-year career, the graduates of a majority of schools will make at least $6,700 more per year than the average high-school graduate. That is more than enough extra income to make college worthwhile. In the 2013 rankings, Harvey Mudd, a private college with a science and engineering focus, ranks highest. On average, its graduates earn an extra $2.1 million over the span of their careers, which is an annual rate of return of 8.3% on the college investment. In the middle of the rankings, Georgia State alumni earn an extra $457,000 for a return on investment of 4.3%. Over half of the nearly 1,500 colleges have a return on investment of over 5%, and only 28 have negative returns. When you account for grants and financial aid, these numbers look even better.

This analysis is not the last word on the financial value of higher education. A generous financial aid package can turn average financial returns into spectacular results. And the choice of major shapes graduates' earnings as much as the school they attend: On average, engineers make $1.8 million more over their careers than someone working in the health support sector. But the basic message appears sound: The extra income college graduates make should more than offset the cost of tuition.

The Payscale analysis, however, does not account for student debt. Most students cannot pay for their education up front. Could loan payments eat up all the returns to college?

One way to answer this question is to look at what percent of their salary graduates spend paying back their loans. If a 25 year-old account manager spends 50% of her salary paying off student loans, that is completely unsustainable. She could never pay both her loan debt and her ordinary expenses. But if she spends 5% of her salary, that would be manageable. The non-profit FinAid considers anything below 10% acceptable; it considers 15% of one's salary the maximum amount a graduate should spend paying off loans.

If we look at how much indebted graduates spend paying off student loans, we find that, on average, their debt is sustainable. It's rare for graduates to spend less than 4% of their salary paying off loans. But graduates of the vast majority of schools spend a sustainable 4%-8% of their salary paying back their loans. And graduates of every American college and university on average spend less than FinAid's upper limit of 15% on loan payments.

All this analysis suggests that college graduates can afford their education. Yet they don't show whether the financial value of college is declining over time. Could the value of a college degree be falling rapidly?

One way to answer this question, at least on a macro level, is to look at data from sources like the U.S. Census. The Census asks about Americans' financial situation as well as their education status. By comparing the difference in salaries between high school graduates and college graduates, researchers can see how the returns to college have risen or fallen over time. The surprising answer is that college has never been a better investment.

Pundits often grouch that the ubiquity of college graduates has rendered a bachelor's degree meaningless, but researchers examining national data in a paper for the National Bureau of Economic Research find the opposite. Despite the increasing number of college graduates, the value of a college degree has only increased over time. In the early 1980s, the average bachelor's degree holder earned 45% more per year than the average high school graduate. Even as the number of college graduates steadily increased, that wage premium increased to 70% in the late 1990s and to nearly 80% today. The authors even speculate that the supply of college graduates is too low.

The story here is that of rising income inequality in the United States. According to one common explanation, technology has increased demand for skilled labor, rewarding college graduates and hurting those without college experience. So while the value of a college degree is increasing, macroeconomic forces — not improvements within higher education — are largely responsible.

Further, the average income of bachelor degree holders grew for decades but stagnated over the past 10 years. This means that the growing payoff of earning a degree over the last decade is a result of the collapse of unskilled laborers' wages. This makes college graduates relatively better off, but it is hardly a rousing defense of higher education.

Still, the data all points to the financial logic of attending college, even in the midst of the current weak economy. Among today's young graduates, 50% are either unemployed or working jobs that don't require a degree. Despite the bum deal of graduating during a recession, however, young graduates in 2010 still enjoyed an unemployment rate of 9.3% compared to the terrible 22.5% unemployment rate faced by Americans of the same age with only a high school degree. The Hamilton Project, a think tank, finds that the extra income young graduates make compared to young high school graduates has grown over time — from $4,000 a year (adjusted for inflation) in the 1980s to $12,000 today.

Skeptics might counter that a college degree seems worth it only because smart, high-achieving people all go to college. Or that college's true value is the expensive piece of paper that signals intelligence and motivation to employers.

These are important points. But the available evidence does suggest that while both critiques have teeth, they account for only part of the increased earnings of college graduates. A number of studies — from comparisons of twins of different education levels to investigations of the increased earnings of those who attend college without graduating — suggest a college education itself leads to increased earnings.

The student loan crisis, however, is not a myth. Both debt burdens and delinquency rates have increased steadily over the past decade. So why do so many students fail to reap the benefits of what seems to be such a sound investment?

Four Theories of Student Loan Defaults

Before we discuss what could be driving high default rates, we should note what is not responsible.

Entitled Millennials pursuing useless liberal arts majors and expecting a plush job to reward their knowledge of Plato and Pointillism does not account for the debt crisis.

As of 2008, the average undergraduate worked 30 hours a week. Undergraduates also focus intensely on preparing for the job market. Nearly half study business, economics, science, technology, engineering, or mathematics. The rest mob programs linked to jobs, like law school and nursing programs. Only 12% study the humanities — and usually find careers, as they always have, in business, law, and the many fields that demand writing or artistic skills.

Nor can we ascribe the student loan crisis to a temporary result of the most recent recession. It certainly contributed. More students decided to ride out the recession in college and state budget crises resulted in reduced subsidies at public universities. But the trends of increased college spending, tuitions, debt, and default all pre-date the recession.

So what explains this paradox that the financial returns to college have never been higher, yet more students than ever are indebted and defaulting on loans?

One possibility is that the data is deceiving us. Since we cannot predict the future, researchers inevitably look backward to calculate the returns to college. In the 1970s, research suggested that college was a losing proposition economically. But college students who ignored that advice benefitted as the economic value of a college degree increased over the course of their careers. We could face the opposite situation today.

While this is a good reminder to view calculations of the 40 year payoff of college with skepticism, it does not seem to explain the paradox. Available research shows the financial payoff of a degree increasing.

A second theory is that while college is on average a sound investment, rising costs mean that college is no longer worth it for an increasing number of students for whom the returns of attending college were already close to zero. And for every student, as debt burdens go up, the chances of defaulting increase as well.

Could all this focus on averages hide a huge number of struggling students on the margins? Researchers criticize the government and colleges for not providing the data to answer this question precisely. But some research suggests that the returns to college are so high that almost all students benefit. One recent study compared the earnings of students who just made the academic cutoff to attend the Florida State University System with those of students who fell just below the cutoff (and mostly did not attend college as a result). We might expect these students to struggle with student debt, yet they reaped returns of 11% from attending college.

A third, complementary explanation is the rise of "merit aid." Colleges sometimes use merit aid to compete for top students, but they increasingly use it to shore up their finances by attracting average students who can pay more tuition. This is especially true at state schools looking to attract nonresident students who will pay higher, out-of-state tuition costs. More merit aid means that an increasing share of aid goes to students who don't need it: The percentage of grants awarded to students in the lowest income percentile dropped from 34% in 1996 to 25% in 2012. The end result is that college becomes more expensive for low-income students, who are most at risk of defaulting on their student loans.

A fourth and final theory is that low profile, inexpensive, poorly performing schools are responsible for the lion's share of defaulting graduates and delinquent debt. The main evidence for this theory is the context of who holds delinquent student debt.

The unemployed law school graduate facing a six

figure student loan debt makes headlines. But student debt in default consists primarily of debts of one to several thousand dollars. Its holders are mostly individuals from low-income families who dropped out of college or even failed to complete high school and took on student debt for a nondegree training program. A disproportionate number are Hispanic or African-American.

So while big name schools are behind the spending race driving up tuition prices, the student debt crisis is best understood by looking at little known universities, community colleges, and even training programs. The schools with the highest reported default rates fit this description: they are local schools, tuition is only a few thousand dollars, and nearly half of the students receive Pell grants (federal grants for low-income students) supplemented by loans.

The rise of for-profit universities has likely fueled this. Good data on for-profits is scarce, but we know that for-profits now enroll 10% of all students, up from 3% in 1999, and account for a quarter of federal aid money. Not all for-profits deserve scorn, but many have drawn scrutiny for terrible graduation and default rates. The dominant business model is to receive accreditation by buying a non-profit college, aggressively market degrees of limited utility (including online accreditation) to low-income students and returning veterans, and then suck up their federal student aid money. Half of all student loans at the for-profit Corinthian Colleges fail, although the colleges still get their federally backed loan payments. The Corinthian Colleges enroll over 100,000 students.

The student debt crisis has fueled anxiety in middle-class families. But the real victims seem to be low-income students who drop out at disproportionately higher rates and attend training programs and lesser known colleges of questionable value.

Is There a Bubble?

The recession, high tuition costs, increasing default rates, and $1 trillion in outstanding student debt have led to a flurry of articles, reports, and sound bites that use the most feared words in America: "crisis" and "bubble."

Student loans, however, seem unlikely to cause a 2008 style collapse of the financial system. As former Federal Reserve Chairman Ben Bernanke has noted, student loans don't threaten the entire financial system because the government is liable for the majority of the debt — not banks. Out of the $1 trillion student loan debt, the federal government guarantees around $850 billion. Nearly half of the remaining $150 billion is held by Sallie Mae, a previously public institution that performs minimal banking activities.

Nor are the rising prices people pay for college based on irrational optimism or divorced from intrinsic value — the essence of a bubble. Despite the gloomy pronouncements, the value of a college degree has increased over time. The data indicates that it is a sound investment — better than the stock market, corporate bonds, and the housing market, according to research by The Hamilton Group — and that there may even be an undersupply of college graduates.

Grading America's Colleges

This does not mean that we should give American higher education a pass. Not bringing down the entire financial system is not a high standard. And the high delinquency rate suggests a serious waste of public and private money.

The skills-bias of technology over the past 30 years has been a gift for colleges, making a college degree increasingly valuable. College graduates could have reaped the benefits of increasing returns to college. This could have also made public subsidies less necessary. Instead, colleges ramped up spending, largely unproductively, necessitating a flood of government subsidies and unnecessary student debt burdens.

The human toll and bad investments represented by the high delinquency rate may represent the actions of certain colleges with particularly poor graduation and default rates. Or colleges' profligacy may be increasing the risk of default across all institutions and pushing students on the margins of benefitting financially from their education toward negative returns. Either way, high college spending is a drag on the economy and a terrible burden on young graduates.

For American colleges, a 'D' is still a passing grade. Despite recent disillusionment, Americans need to know that — on average — a college degree is still a very sound investment. But they also should know that most colleges have performed poorly at providing value to their students. The fact that college is still a sound investment should not keep us from demanding better of the purveyors of lofty speeches about human progress. Nor blind us to the possibility of challenging the four year degree system.

College may seem at a glance to be too much of a four year party. But don't simply blame the students. For an increasing number of them, it's a party they'd rather skip. Because after graduation, the party continues for the colleges. Only the graduates endure the long hangover, and, between the graduates' debt and taxpayer subsidies, we all foot the bill.

PART III:
THE BUSINESS OF MANIPULATION

"You know, I know this steak doesn't exist. I know that when I put it in my mouth, the Matrix is telling my brain that it is juicy and delicious. After nine years, you know what I realize? Ignorance is bliss."

(Cypher, *The Matrix*)

12.

HOW MARKETERS INVENTED BODY ODOR

In the mid 1990s, the executives at consumer goods company Procter & Gamble thought they had developed a new hit product. Thanks to several million dollars of research, they had created a spray that could eliminate odors. They called it Febreze.

To roll out the new creation, Procter & Gamble (P&G) assembled a marketing team that put together ads showing relieved customers taking deep breaths of fresh air after spraying Febreze on jackets that reeked of cigarette smoke and sofas that stank of wet dog. As related by journalist Charles Duhigg in The Power of Habit, confidence in the product and advertisements ran so high that the team started planning for promotions and bonuses as they launched the advertising campaign.

After a few weeks, excitement turned to alarm. Febreze did not fly off the shelves; it was barely selling. The P&G executives were alarmed, and the marketing team struggled to figure out what they had done wrong. The epiphany came at the home of a crazy cat lady. Duhigg elaborates:

When P.& G.'s scientists walked into her living room, where her nine cats spent most of their time, the scent was so overpowering that one of them gagged. According to Stimson, who led the Febreze team, a researcher asked the woman, "What do you do about the cat smell?"

"It's usually not a problem," she said.

"Do you smell it now?"

"No," she said. *"Isn't it wonderful? They hardly smell at all!"*

Febreze had failed, the marketers realized, because people had no idea that they needed the product. People generally adjust to bad smells in everyday life until they no longer notice them. Had Procter and Gamble studied the experience of deodorant companies eighty years earlier, the company might have been better prepared for the challenges of marketing Febreze.

In 1912, an Ohio high school student named Edna Murphey attempted to sell an antiperspirant invented by her father, a surgeon. As an article in Smithsonian Magazine recounts, her father used it to keep his hands dry during surgeries while Murphey found it prevented sweating and odor in her armpits. Murphey called the company Odorono, a word meaning, "Odor? Oh no!"

The product had it share of problems. It could stain clothing red — one woman's wedding dress was a victim — and irritate the skin. But it was an improvement over practices at the time. On particularly hot days, women might use "dress shields," which were simply cotton or rubber pads, to prevent sweat from soaking clothing.

But as with Febreze, deodorant solved a problem no one felt they had. People believed regular baths to be sufficient. Men found odor masculine; women used perfume to cover up any smells. Worst of all, in the Victorian culture of the time, talking about bodily functions or sweaty armpits publicly was taboo. During a long, sticky summer of hawking the deodorant from a trade booth, Murphey struggled to sell her product. So the plucky high school student took the meager profits she made selling Odorono at the 1912 Atlantic city exposition and hired a copywriter from the J. Walter Thompson Company, an ad agency.

What came next, Sarah Everts explains in Smithsonian, was a marketing coup. After several years of muddling success, the young copywriter, James Young, decided to convince women that they smelled. A first ad, "Within the Curve of a Woman's arm," read:

> "A woman's arm! Poets have sung of it, great artists have painted its beauty. It should be the daintiest, sweetest thing in the world. And yet, unfortunately, it isn't always."

As Everts writes, his ads suggested to women that they "may be stinky and offensive, and they might not even know it... If [they] wanted to keep a man, [they'd] better not smell." In other words, Young tried to convince every woman that she was the oblivious cat lady and that the rest of the world was the Febreze marketing team, running off to gag at the smell.

The ad shocked. Young's female co-workers stopped talking to him and women cancelled subscriptions to magazines running the ad. But it worked. Sales doubled, then rose above a million dollars per year. "Within the Curve of a Woman's arm" is considered a classic in marketing, an ad that launched the Advertising Hall of Fame career of James Young. Once deodorant companies pulled the same trick on men —

convincing them that their manly odors could get them canned from their desk jobs and putting deodorant in whiskey bottles so it didn't seem wussy — they had the entire population spending billions to use their products every day.

Procter & Gamble, on the other hand, solved its problem by marketing Febreze as an air freshener. Although aerosols and other fresheners had long existed, good marketing combined with P&G's market dominance propelled sales. Eventually, P&G began to tell people again that Febreze eliminated odors, which was now recast as a differentiating feature from other fragrant aerosols. Through the trojan horse of an air freshener, Febreze became a bestseller and anti-odor sprays became a major product.

Odorono and P&G faced a similar problem — their products solved a problem that people either did not have or did not recognize. In response, they took opposite paths to success. The marketers of Febreze changed the connotation of their product from negative to positive. The image of Febreze went from stinky couches to gleaming kitchens, from dealing with bad smells to spraying a nice scent after a morning of cleaning the house. The marketers of deodorant told the world that everyone was gossipping about how bad their armpits smelled.

One campaign went positive and the other negative, and they both worked. But it may be telling that while the Febreze campaign relied on the brute force of a Fortune 500 company's resources, the Odorono campaign turned the project of a Cincinnati high school student into a multimillion dollar company.

13.

THE WORLD'S MOST EXPENSIVE FREE CREDIT REPORT

In 2005, the credit monitoring company Experian paid $925,000 to settle charges that the company deceived consumers. Experian had advertised a "free credit report" on its website, Consumerinfo.com, but it actually charged consumers $79.95 for the service — a fact that was buried in the fine print. The Federal Trade Commission (FTC), the federal agency in charge of regulating truth in advertising, announced the settlement in a press release and declared victory on behalf of consumers.

But Experian kept at it. The company disregarded the FTC's warning and continued to charge customers $79.95 for a credit report it implied was "free" on Consumerinfo.com. So, in 2007, the FTC issued another triumphant press release that proclaimed that this time it really had stopped those roguish fellows at Experian. The company would have to pay a $300,000 settlement for violating the FTC's prior ruling.

But in 2007, even as it was settling the second reprimand from the FTC, Experian poured tens of millions of dollars into a television advertising campaign for FreeCreditReport.com," a new website. The campaign's centerpiece was a television commercial featuring a band that literally sang the praises of checking credit scores online for free. The only price mentioned in the ads was "free," which was sung loudly and written prominently on the screen.

How could a website offering a "free credit report" afford expensive television advertisements? Well, if you listened closely, you could hear a barely audible voice whisper at the end of the commercial, "Offer requires enrollment in Triple Advantage."

As you may suspect, enrolling in "Triple Advantage" wasn't free. Experian provided a complimentary credit report, but it bundled it with an on-going credit monitoring service for which it charged customers $19.99 a month. People who signed up would be charged in perpetuity until they noticed and figured out how to cancel the charges before the seven day grace period ended. Experian gave away its credit report for free, but then laughed all the way to the bank while collecting "monitoring fees."

One person duped by Experian summarizes the whole situation in this very typical online complaint:

> "This company is a scam. Beware. They were billing me [repeatedly] without any authorization. Another example of the degradation of business practices in the US. When a capitalist society turns to deceit for financial gain, everybody loses. I am ashamed to have fought for this country."

But how could Experian perpetrate the same deceptive ploy over and over, only to receive minor fines from the FTC? Well, the FTC can't technically fine a company for lying. The FTC can tell companies to cease and desist a deceptive marketing technique, or to stop burying important information in a footnote — but it can only levy fines on companies that continue to do so after the warning. Or, as with the case of Experian, the FTC can go to court and file a civil case against the company that may result in a modest settlement. However, a determined company can launch a different — if very similar and equally misleading — advertisement to evade FTC sanction. It's a cat and mouse game between the FTC and companies like Experian that bend the truth in increasingly creative ways.

And the upside of distorting the truth can be enormous. The FreeCreditReport.com advertising campaign was a profit bonanza for Experian. Over twenty million consumers fell for this "free credit report" gambit, which generated hundreds of millions of dollars that Experian could reinvest into even more television ads for the service to attract even more victims. At its peak, the company spent $70 million dollars a year advertising FreeCreditReport.com. The commercials were so ubiquitous that the actors in the commercials became minor celebrities.

The public soon realized that FreeCreditReport.com wasn't actually so "free" and started looking for alternatives. In another masterstroke, Experian launched a second website called FreeCreditScore.com and heavily advertised it as well. This produced the illusion of a competing credit report website taking on the jerks at FreeCreditReport.com, when Experian really owned both sites.

Ultimately, in 2009, Congress had to step in and pass a law that prohibited companies from claiming to offer a "free credit report" if they really were not. While one might congratulate Congress for diligently protecting the American consumer, lawmakers also added an unrelated amendment to the bill that made it legal to carry firearms in national parks. So, thank you

Congress?

Experian finally stopped charging for "free" credit reports; instead of offering a "free" credit report on FreeCreditReport.com, Experian now offers a $1 credit report. When you pay this $1, however, Experian mysteriously enrolls you in a monthly credit monitoring service that costs $19.99 a month. Ah, you got us again Experian. We just can't quit you.

Worst of all, since 2003, customers have had the right to a truly free credit report at the government website AnnualCreditReport.com. As required by federal law, the site is "brought to you by" the three major credit reporting companies: TransUnion, Equifax, and Experian. The site warns visitors that "Lots of sites promise credit reports for free. AnnualCreditReport.com is the only official site explicitly directed by Federal law to provide them."

Profit margins are destiny. The companies with the most lucrative business models can afford ads that attract the most customers. When deception increases profit margins, dishonest companies crowd out the honest competitors or free services that can't afford to market themselves as widely. Since it's much more lucrative to charge customers absurd fees than give away a free report, you're much more likely to find out about FreeCreditReport.com through television commercials and premium ads in Google search results. Beware the company that has a lot of money to spend on ads.

Today, Experian is a publicly traded company worth over $10 billion. The Queen of England recently knighted the company's Chairman and CEO (who now goes by the name Sir John Peace) for "services to business and the voluntary sector."

So abusing your customers' trust is not only profitable, but it might earn you a spot in the aristocracy. And while Experian paid a measly $1.2 million settlement for its shenanigans with Consumerinfo.com, it was never once fined for the epic rip-off that was FreeCreditReport.com.

As of 2014, Experian reports it will begin phasing out the word "free" in the branding of its credit report products. In their latest financial reporting, company executives mention that this might "constrain revenue growth" this year.

14.

WHAT HAPPENS TO
DONATED CARS?

Asbestos law firms. Personal injury attorney. Donating a used car. Online auto insurance.

What do all these things have in common? They are among the most expensive keywords available on Google Adwords.

This means that there is something very valuable about placing an ad in the search results for these phrases. To place an advertisement within some results, Google charges as little as five cents per click. For keywords like "online auto insurance", however, Google charges from $60 to $110 per click.

Companies pay so much for these placements because each person that clicks on the ad has a good chance of making the company a lot of money. A sick patient interested in suing over asbestos poisoning represents a potential jackpot for a law firm. Auto insurance companies can make good money in perpetuity by signing up a new client. But what is so lucrative about car donations?

Google search results are not the only place where car donations are advertised. On billboards, in newspapers, and on the radio, charities exhort people to donate their old car in return for a tax write-off. They promise a win-win: easily get rid of an old car at a good rate, and help support charity.

Born out of an IRS policy that imagined the occasional car being donated to a family in need or a nonprofit that could use some wheels, the tax write-off for car donations has spawned a market worth hundreds of millions or perhaps billions of dollars. Hundreds of thousands of Americans donate their used cars every year to charities, or more frequently, to for-profit companies that sell them and return a portion of the proceeds to charity. But the portion that is donated is often very small, raising the question of whether car donations fund charity or subsidize a surprisingly lucrative business.

A Multi-Billion Dollar Industry

The tax write-off for cars is part of a much larger IRS policy that makes noncash contributions to charities tax deductible. The intent is to incentivize donating an old boat for use in oceanography research, old clothes to Goodwill, or a used car for a charity's use.

In 1978, the Goodwill of the greater Washington D.C. area initiated a car donation drive as a way to raise funds. Instead of accepting cars that it could use or give away, Goodwill sold the cars and put the proceeds toward its general budget. Charities across the country soon copied its creative use of the tax code. The IRS does not regularly collect statistics on car donations, but press coverage makes clear that the practice was popular and growing in the nineties. By 2000, Americans claimed $654 million in annual tax exemptions on the basis of car donations. That represented 733,000 tax returns, or .06% of all tax claims, donating a car for an average exemption of $890.

The car donation process goes as follows: Donors contact charities, often in response to advertisements that highlight the tax write-off. The charity asks screening questions about the car (sometimes to make sure that the sale will be profitable, but many charities accept even the worst clunker to engender goodwill) and then pays a tow truck to pick it up from the donor's home and take it to an auto auction lot where it is sold. The donor transfers the title of ownership and receives paperwork proving her donation.

This paperwork allows donors to reduce their tax liability. If someone donates a car worth $2,500, she cannot reduce her tax liability by $2,500. Instead, the amount deducted reflects one's tax bracket. In 2013, an individual with a yearly income from $87,850 to $183,250 was taxed at a rate of 28%. So, if Americans lower their taxes by about $654 million per year, they donate over $2 billion worth of cars.

Despite the multi-billion dollar scale of car donations, the U.S. General Accounting Office, when it reported on the practice in 2003, found that only 4,300 major charities (those with annual revenues above $100,000) had car donation programs — less than 3% of such charities.

One reason that few charities pursue what seems to be a significant pool of funding is that charities receive relatively little of the money written off Americans' taxes for car donations. In 2003, the General Accounting Office followed the donation of 54 vehicles to car donation drives and found that the amount received by charity for most of the vehicles was "five percent or less of the value donors claimed as a deduction on their tax returns."

Some of that "lost" money reflects the costs of running car donation drives. But it mostly reflects how people claimed deductions for more than their car actually sold for.

IRS guidelines encouraged donors to use independent resources to estimate the value of their car and therefore their tax write-off. But those guidelines were written to reflect people donating goods that charities would use directly. With the innovation of charities selling donated cars rather than using the cars themselves, the assumption that charities received value equal to the value of the car no longer held. To quickly sell cars, charities sold them at auction, where they received a lower price than they would if owners spent time searching for a buyer willing to pay the full market value of the car.

In response, the IRS began requiring in 2005 that donors of cars valued higher than $500 receive a receipt detailing how much their car actually sold for at auction and then claim a deduction on their taxes based on that price. Despite this reform, car donations remain an inefficient means of transferring money to charities. A 2005 report (on data from the first year after the IRS reform) from the California Attorney General found that only half of the proceeds of car donation drives accrued to charities. The disappearance of the other half is explained by the rise of for-profit car donation fundraisers.

Selling Cars is a Full Time Job

The charities benefitting from car donation drives include Susan G. Komen for the Cure, the largest and most well-funded breast cancer organization in the United States, and the Purple Heart Foundation, which assists American veterans and their families. A minority of charities raise most of their funding from car donations, and therefore deal with most to all of the donation process themselves. But the majority see it as one of many revenue streams and prefer to outsource as much of the car donation process as possible.

As car donation drives proliferated, private companies offering to raise money through car donations popped up. These companies have names like Car Donation Services and Car Program (LLC). They take care of every aspect of the donation, from advertising to speaking to the donor to picking up the car and selling it. In return for their services, they retain a portion of the profits.

People donating their cars to charity rarely realize that a private company is involved. The company websites look like a nonprofit's. They feature pictures of veterans, breast cancer awareness walks, or smiling children, the names of the charities for which they raise money, and the language of charitable giving. Their customer service representatives maintain the fiction of working for a charity when they talk to donors on the phone.

There are no laws that regulate third party car donation services, other than requirements in less than a quarter of states that they fill out certifying paperwork or contribute regular financial disclosures. The government merely recommends that people "be generous and informed donors."

Given that the government subsidizes these private companies in the form of the charitable tax deductions for donors, the companies' legitimacy would seem to rest on how well they fundraise for the charities they represent. The verdict is decidedly mixed.

Some of the only data available comes from the Office of the California Attorney General. California requires commercial fundraisers in the state to file financial reports, and the Office of the Attorney General has released reports on the percentage of profits going to charities.

In 2001, private car donation services in California raised $45.8 million in gross proceeds from car auctions. (Gross in the sense of the "profit" left after the company paid operational expenses.) Of that, charities received $16 million — about 35 percent. In 2005, after the IRS rule change, charities actually did better, receiving 49.03% or $17.02 million of the $34.72 million raised.

Is it exorbitant for a commercial fundraiser to take 50% of gross proceeds? Reports from national and local government express scorn at 50% takes, and not without reason. That 50% figure comes after fundraisers have already paid themselves fees, so the full share of car sales captured by for-profit fundraising companies is much higher than 50%.

What these averages may cover up, however, is that the percentage of proceeds given to charities by more civic-minded companies could disguise the greedy actions of others. State Attorney Generals investigating car donation practices, as well as the Better Business Bureau, have reported on corporations that give charities only a small, flat rate per car sold or a cut dramatically lower than 50%. The California Attorney General's 2001 data showed that the cut of proceeds given to charities by private companies ranged from 2% to 80%. The companies that keep most of the money for themselves are likely the ones that can bid $85 for a visitor from Google.

The Nonprofit Profiteers

Just as private companies popped up to run car donation schemes for charities that cannot or do not want to sell donated cars themselves, a number of large nonprofits that focus on selling used cars to fundraise for charities have been founded as well. This is generally good news for charities, as a nonprofit fundraiser can pass on all of its gross proceeds to the charities it represents. But there is good reason to believe that many large nonprofit fundraising organizations may be more interested in paying fees to themselves than maximizing their contributions to charity.

One of the organizations that advertises in Google search results for the phrase "donate a car" is Cars-FightingCancer.org. The website has pictures of cancer survivors undergoing chemotherapy and the pink ribbon that represents breast cancer awareness. It also proudly states that it is an official IRS 501-C3 charity. Only with some digging can a viewer discover that Cars Fighting Cancer is part of the nonprofit Others First Inc.

The Better Business Bureau advises donors to regard Others First with extreme caution. The nonprofit pays 30% of its proceeds to consulting companies owned by Rick Frazier, a man who ran several defunct car donation companies that charities accused of fraud. "The Virginia-based Military Order of the Purple Heart Foundation alleged in a court suit that an audit found widespread problems with Frazier's role in that program," the BBB writes, "including self-dealing, illegal practices and destruction of incriminating records." Nevertheless, Others First has deals with many charities to run donation drives in their name, some worth tens of millions of dollars.

Kars 4 Kids, a nonprofit that raises nearly $30 million annually and advertises on Google and on nationwide radio, also demonstrates how easily organizations can mislead donors. Although the Kars 4 Kids website speaks of work benefiting disadvantaged children, it is actually an assumed name of Oorah Inc., a charity that "provides religious education for kids of non-observant Jews." It is only the largest of several organizations pulling in millions of dollars from car donations in New York whose proceeds go toward exclusively religious purposes under the guise of more standard charitable work.

It is also not uncommon for sham charities to make

millions from car donations without donating a single penny. In 2010, Shoba Bakhsh, the head of "Hope for the Disabled Kids, Inc.," pled guilty to charges of fraud. She received $2 million in donations over two years, but did not contribute any to charity. She simply forged testimonials from local hospitals that made it seem as if they received support from Hope for the Disabled Kids.

The New York Attorney General discovered Bakhsh's fraud during an investigation into car donation drives. While it may seem like her clumsy operation would inevitably be discovered, many other frauds may go undetected for years. The IRS does not audit the deductions taxpayers claim for donating vehicles — instead prioritizing larger scale deductions — so there is no one to check that tax deductions actually benefit charity. Nor do attorney generals in most states regularly investigate car donation companies and nonprofits. The only way for a fraud to be caught is for a suspicious donor to refer it to the state attorney general. Until then, faux charities can continue to bring in "donations."

Fundraising for Profit

Although its ubiquitous ads make it stand out, the ecosystem surrounding the donated car tax write-off — from legitimate, if not terribly efficient, fundraising efforts to outright fraud — represents just one part of the private sector's questionable role in fundraising for nonprofits.

The reason private companies (or shady nonprofits) can give charities such a small cut of the funds they raise is that the charities often have no incentive to hold the commercial fundraisers accountable. While big name charities have leverage over commercial partners and closely monitor their reputations, the majority of nonprofits are small organizations with limited capacity and a desperate need of funds. When a company or nonprofit offers to provide them with more funding in exchange for signing a contract, they have no reason to refuse. As one of countless nonprofits, they have little leverage to negotiate a larger cut of the proceeds., and given that the fundraising company has no legal requirement to disclose its profits or inner workings, charities may have no idea how many cars the fundraiser sells in their name and no reason to question the modest size of the checks they receive.

These same incentives are at work for companies that offer to solicit donations over the phone and on street corners on behalf of charities. Just like with car donation services, private telemarketers and canvassers cut deals with nonprofits to fundraise in their name. When they solicit donations from people, they act like part of the charity and make no mention of their quotas and commissions.

A report from the state of Washington found that charities received 46% of funds raised by commercial fundraisers. A 2009 Charity Navigator analysis of states that require disclosures wrote that the companies in each state contributed an average of 32 to 59 percent of the proceeds to charity, and that the costs of running telemarketing and canvassing campaigns ate up much of the charitable contributions made by donors. Most years New York releases a "Pennies for Charity" report on commercial fundraising. It regularly finds that charities receive less than 50% of the proceeds of the fundraising performed by private telemarketers and canvassers. In 2011, it reported that "63%, or $157 million of the funds raised by 81 telemarketers was paid to fundraisers for fees and/or used to cover the costs of conducting the campaigns."

With well over half of the money raised going to the private fundraising companies, donors' money and tax write-offs seem to be furthering the goal of keeping telemarketers and canvassers employed more than the goals of supporting veterans and advancing cancer research. No national level data exists on commercial fundraising, but with New York State alone bringing in hundreds of millions of dollars every year, the market is easily worth billions.

Charity for Whom?

An IRS loophole has created a quirky situation where charities are in the business of acquiring and selling used cars. Charities can make some money from car donations and often outsource selling donated cars and other aspects of fundraising. By doing so, they can focus on their programming: running after school programs, sending care packages to soldiers overseas, or running awareness and outreach events for terminal illnesses.

But car donation drives, along with other forms of commercial fundraising like telemarketing and canvassing, seem to be an inefficient means of supporting charitable work. Less than half of the proceeds accrue to charities, with private companies retaining the rest, and fees eat up over half of the value of the donations. This not only means that people support charities less than they intend, it also deprives the U.S. government of revenue.

Since the IRS neither audits nor compiles any data on these tax deductions and commercial fundraisers, we also don't know how many fundraising organizations, whether for-profit or nonprofit, exaggerate their expenses or even commit outright fraud. In many instances, it doesn't seem that charities make an informed decision to get into the car donation game. Instead, charities shrug their shoulders when approached by predatory private companies and lend them the charitable mirage they need in exchange for modest contributions to their budget.

There is no law against profiting off fundraising for charities. It is up to donors to do their research and donate in a way that will maximize the support they provide for charities. But how much of people's donations and tax write-offs have to go toward private companies' fees and salaries to reach the point that it is charity for the companies, not the causes they claim to support?

15.

THE INVENTION OF
THE CHILEAN SEA BASS

The Chilean sea bass is not the type of fish you find on the menu at Red Lobster or Long John Silver's. Instead, you're more likely to choose it out of a lineup that includes filet mignon and lobster risotto — and to pay top dollar for its buttery, melt in your mouth flavor.

Given its name, which conjures up exotic notions of South American fisherman carefully acquiring this prized fish off the coast of Chile, the price may seem appropriate. But only a minority of Chilean sea bass come from the coast of Chile. Many fish sold under the name hail from arctic regions. Moreover, the fish isn't even a type of bass; it's a cod. Until 1977, the name Chilean sea bass didn't exist, and few people ate the fish before the 1990s. Prior to that, scientists knew the fish by the less mouthwatering name of the Patagonian or Antarctic toothfish.

In short, the Chilean sea bass is a pure marketing invention — and a wildly successful one. Far from unique, the story of the Chilean sea bass represents something of a formula in today's climate of overfishing: choose a previously ignored fish, give it a more appealing name, and market it. With a little luck, a fish once tossed back as bycatch will become part of trendy $50 dinners.

From Fish Sticks to the Four Seasons

Despite the oceans' vast size, our appetite for their endowments appears even stronger.

Collecting data on the state of fish populations is expensive and difficult enough to leave room for debate. That debate, however, is generally between doom and gloom like marine biologist Daniel Pauly's assertion that we face the "end of fish" and other researchers' cautious optimism about the recovery of some fish stocks. It is the most popular fish that face the lowest supply: Pauly notes that over the past 50 years, cod, swordfish, and bluefin tuna populations have declined by some 90%.

As populations of popular commercial fish dwindled, the seafood industry went further afield, although experts say operations now cover virtually every corner of the globe. Manufacturers turned to bycatch and once-ignored fish like the blue grenadier to make fish sticks and filet-o-fish sandwiches. Beyond fast food, sit-down restaurants, fish markets, and even sushi joints have taken to passing off ignoble fish as their more popular cousins. One study found 20% of fish in America to be mislabeled. The rate was 50% in California.

The seafood industry also tapped new fish to offset the decline in major commercial offerings. In 2009, a Washington Post article on the practice noted, "As they went farther and deeper, fishermen brought back fish that people didn't have recipes — or even words — for." So, the fish received new, more refined names. In the seventies, seafood dealers renamed the slimehead, a fish named for its "distinctive mucus canals," the "orange roughly." Sales of the goosefish — long thrown back by fishermen — skyrocketed in the 1980s and 1990s once rechristened the monkfish. Rebranding sea urchins — once known by Maine lobstermen as "whore's eggs" — under its Japanese name "uni" helped it catch on as a popular sushi ingredient now achieving popularity in other cuisine.

An Exercise in Branding

So how did the toothfish join the ranks of well-branded finds?

As recounted in Hooked: A True Story of Pirates, Poaching and the Perfect Fish, in 1977 an American fish merchant named Lee Lantz was scouring fishing boats in a Chilean port. Lantz's business was finding new types of fish to bring to market, and he became excited when he spotted a menacing looking, five-foot long toothfish that inspired him to ask, "That is one amazing-looking fish. What the hell is it?"

The fishermen had not meant to catch the fish, which no one recognized. But as the use of deep-water longlines became more common, toothfish, which dwell in deep waters, started appearing in markets. Taking it for a type of bass, Lantz believed it would do well in America. But when he tried a bite of the tooth-fish, fried up in oil, it disappointed. It had almost no flavor. Nevertheless, as G. Bruce Knecht, author of *Hooked*, writes:

> *"[Lantz] still thought its attributes were a perfect match for the American market. It had a texture similar to Atlantic cod's, the richness of tuna, the innocuous mild flavor of a flounder, and its fat content made it feel almost buttery in the mouth. Mr. Lantz believed a white-fleshed fish that almost*

> *melted in your mouth — and a fish that did*
> *not taste 'fishy' — could go a very long*
> *way with his customers at home."*

But if the strength of the toothfish (a name Lantz didn't even know — he learned that locals called it "cod of the deep") was its ability to serve as a blank canvas for chefs, it needed a good name. Lantz stuck with calling it a bass, since that would be familiar to Americans. He rejected two of his early ideas for names, Pacific sea bass and South American sea bass, as too generic, according to Knecht. He decided on Chilean sea bass, the specificity of which seemed more exclusive.

Despite its new, noble name, chefs in fancy Manhattan restaurants did not immediately serve a nicely broiled Chilean Sea Bass with Moroccan salsa over couscous. It took a few years for Lantz to land contracts for his new find. Initially, he made only a few small sales to wholesalers and other distributors despite offering samples far and wide. Finally, in 1980, a company struggling with the rising cost of halibut that the company used in its fish sticks bought Lantz's entire stock, banking on people not tasting the difference between halibut and toothfish beneath the deep fry.

From there, Chilean sea bass quickly worked its way up the food chain. Chinese restaurants purchased it as a cheap replacement for black cod (Chilean sea bass is, after all, a type of cod). Celebrity chefs embraced it, enjoying, as Knecht writes, it ability to "hold up to any method of cooking, accept any spice," and never overcook. The Four Seasons first served it in 1990; it was Bon Appetit's dish of the year in 2001.

A Self-Fulfilling Prophecy

Addressing new arrivals to Plymouth Plantation in 1622, Governor William Bradford apologized that all he "could presente their friends with was a lobster... without bread or anything else but a cupp of fair water."

It may seem surprising that previously ignored fish like the toothfish and the slimehead (successfully rebranded as the orange roughy) could so quickly become the toast of the town. But with a long-term perspective, it becomes clear that the line between bycatch and fancy seafood is not a great wall defended by the impregnability of taste, but a porous border susceptible to the effects of supply and demand, technology, and fickle trends. This is true of formerly low-class seafood like oysters and, most of all, the once humble lobster.

In the early colonial days, lobster was a subsistence food. The biggest knock against lobster seems to be how plentiful it was. Food histories like The Encyclopedia of American Food and Drink describe lobsters "washing ashore in two foot piles." As wealth grew in colonial America, lobster remained a food primarily for prisoners, indentured servants, and the poor. Commercial markets were limited and a lobster bake would have had a status roughly equivalent to fast food takeout today.

Lobster seems to have first found a mass market thanks to the advent of canning in the early to mid 1800s. Once canneries managed to convince skeptical Maine fishermen to become lobstermen, canned lobster could be found in inland stores, although still at one fifth the price of baked beans.

But what made the lobster king were 19th century food tourists — moneyed visitors to the New England coast from Philadelphia, New York, and Boston. These "rusticators" came looking for the "Yankee America of Myth," so locals served them lobster for dinner on fine china with butter and herbs. With the advent of refrigeration, rusticators could pay top dollar for this new "luxury" of lobster in urban stores and restaurants as well.

Although lobsters were once cheap and plentiful, and expensive only due to their nostalgic branding, lobster prices soon reflected real rarity. Between canning and the demand for lobster as a luxury purchase, lobstermen overfished. Whereas huge lobsters were once laughably easy to pull up, finding one pound lobsters became the work of a professional. The exclusive image of the lobster became a self-fulfilling prophecy, reflecting its stocks in the real world.

Each of the rebranded fish — the slimehead turned orange roughy, the sea urchin turned uni, the toothfish turned Chilean sea bass — experienced the same. After their successful branding helped make them part of high-brow cuisine, the stocks of each plummeted. Seafood Watch, a sustainable seafood advisory list, released guidelines on each as scientists worried about their possible extinction. In 2002, a mere 10 years after Chilean sea bass became popular, environmental groups teamed up with American chefs on a "Take a Pass on Chilean Sea Bass" campaign that encouraged chefs to take the fish of their menus.

Before the campaign began, international agreements set quotas and established other regulations on the capture and sale of toothfish, but advocates insisted the boycott was necessary given the prevalence of illegal poaching. In 2002, the Commerce Department estimated that 2/3 of Chilean sea bass sales were illegal. The incentives to ignore regulations were simply too high.

This is well illustrated by the case of Antonio Garcia Perez, a Spanish fisherman with serious disregard for fishing regulations. Perez used longlines "that stretch over more than 15 miles and carry up to 15,000 baited hooks" to catch as many as 40 tons of Chilean sea bass in a day. As Knecht recounts in Hooked, Perez instigated "one of the longest pursuits in nautical history" in 2003 while fishing for toothfish near the Heard and McDonald Islands, two barren, volcanic spits of land located roughly equidistant between South Africa, Australia, and Antarctica. Spotted by Australian patrol boats, Perez ordered his ship to flee south toward Antarctica.

Perez's boat, the Viarsa, had 96 tons of Chilean sea bass on board worth $1 million. With an Australian ship giving chase, the Viarsa made directly for a storm of 75 mph winds. Knecht describes the ship ascending building-size waves that rocked the ship, bent the walls, and created "the impression that the hull was being pressed together like an accordion." To protect a cache of a fish no one much cared about a decade earlier, the Viarsa raced 4,000 miles (more than the distance from California to New York) over 3 weeks until additional patrol boats trapped it in the South Atlantic Ocean and took Perez and his crew to an Australian court to face charges of violating Australia's Fisheries Management Act.

Nature, Nurtured

In the United States, the Food and Drug Administration oversees the labeling of seafood. But the agency generally doesn't have a problem with people in the seafood industry marketing fish under new names, focusing instead on cases of fraud and mislabeling that leads to safety concerns. The FDA now recognizes Chilean sea bass as an accepted name along with Patagonian and Antarctic toothfish.

It would be nice if market mechanisms kicked in to protect stocks of popular seafood. When lobster became popular and overfished, the difficulty of trapping them would increase the price, leading people to seek alternatives. Lobsters would have a respite until stocks increased and prices dropped, hopefully leading to a sustainable equilibrium over time.

Unfortunately — as shown by the story of Antonio

Garcia Perez and the world's fishing stocks — nothing of the sort happens. People continue to pay for popular seafood, with high prices becoming a draw for fishermen rather than a deterrent for diners. The result is hard to enforce (and negotiate) regulations and a tragedy of the commons.

The trajectory of the Chilean sea bass — from almost unknown, to fish sticks, to a fine cuisine risking extinction in a mere 20 years — shows just how much power seafood markets hold over the state of our oceans. That said, regulation and campaigns like "Take A Pass On Chilean Sea Bass" have had an effect. Seafood Watch notes the success of some recovering stocks and identifies a number of responsible sources for acquiring toothfish.

In the future, expect to see more examples like the toothfish turned Chilean sea bass. Partly due to chefs and foodies always looking for the hot new thing, but also because in the context of overfishing, we simply need new things to eat.

PART IV:
SUSPENSION OF HUMAN DECENCY

"They were careless people, Tom and Daisy – they smashed up things and creatures and then retreated back into their money or vast carelessness or whatever it was that kept them together, and let other people clean up the mess they had made."

(F. Scott Fitzgerald, *The Great Gatsby*)

16.

WHAT IT'S LIKE TO FAIL

Editor's note: The following is the personal story of David Raether, a former comedy writer for the sitcom Roseanne who later became homeless.

On Christmas Day, 2001, I sat down at my Yamaha G2 grand piano, set up my metronome, and opened up a book of Shostakovich's "Preludes."

It was late afternoon, and the warm, orange light of the fading day poured into my five-bedroom house — paid for by my $300,000 a year income as a Hollywood comedy writer — in San Marino, California, a wealthy suburb of Los Angeles. My wife, Marina, was cooking dinner for me and our eight children, and it was as happy a Christmas afternoon as I would ever have.

***

On Christmas morning, 2008, I woke up on the floor of the 1997 Chrysler minivan I lived in, parked behind the Kinko's just two miles from my old house in San Marino. It was raining, and I was cold, even though I had slept in three layers of clothes. It was one of those blustery storms that regularly whoosh down from the

Gulf of Alaska and pummel Los Angeles during the winter. I climbed out of the van and walked to a Starbucks five blocks away. Although I didn't have any money, I had scavenged the Sunday *Los Angeles Times* crossword puzzle from another coffeehouse a couple days before. The baristas didn't mind me sitting quietly for several hours every day to warm up and kill time.

I was neither a drug addict nor an alcoholic, nor was I a criminal. But I had committed one of the more basic of American sins: I had failed. In eight years, my career had vanished, then my savings, and then our home. My family broke apart. I was alone, hungry, and defeated.

Between 2007 and 2011, some five million American families lost their homes to foreclosure.

Some of them found alternative housing by renting an apartment or moving in with family members. But not all of them. Many American families broke apart during this time. Mine was one of them. And I was one of the people who ended up homeless. This, however, is not the story of five million American families. This is just my story.

Our family faced the same economic forces that hurt many families, but I don't blame the banks or politicians or anyone else for what happened to us. I made a thousand decisions, large and small, that seemed reasonable at the time but cumulatively led to our situation. It is tempting to blame external forces for the disasters that befall us, but as Shakespeare wrote in "Julius Ceasar," the fault for what happens to us "is not in our stars but in ourselves."

It was Christmas. I stared out the Starbucks window at the rain. God, help me. I had said this prayer a thousand times, and would say it a thousand more. I had to find a way back to my life.

And over the course of the next four years, I would do just that. I would do it with the pure, unquenchable, unrelenting — some might say naïve — belief that things would work out. And I would do it through Craigslist, the omnifariously oddball website that has nearly destroyed the newspaper industry by taking over the classified advertising business. But it would be Craigslist that would help me find my way back.

People say you can find just about anything you need on Craigslist. You might even find your life again.

***

My fall was all the harder because I had my dream job. You know, the job you dreamt of as a little kid: quarterback in the NFL, supermodel, astronaut... Something crazy and cool that hardly anybody is lucky or talented enough to land.

It all started like this: I was maybe six years old and watching "The Ed Sullivan Show." Ed Sullivan thanked the last performer and then turned to the audience and said, "Ladies and gentlemen, Alan King!" A burly, handsome man walked alone onto the stage in a dark suit and tie and began talking. And he was funny! And the audience was laughing. I was enthralled. It seemed like magic. The next morning, I came downstairs for breakfast and told my mother I wanted to write jokes for a living. *"Oh, no, you're not going to do that!"* she said. *"That's just foolishness."*

This convinced me that this was something I absolutely wanted to do with my life.

A couple of decades later, I took time off from my budding career as a newspaper man to travel around Europe. While in Germany, I met a beautiful and mysterious Serbian poet named Marina. We met by accident, but we latched on to each other with a ferocious and unstoppable kind of love. We got married a year later.

Suddenly reality came crashing. I was married and needed a real job. I decided to launch a magazine in

Minneapolis with a friend from college. We made two basic mistakes: First, the magazine wasn't very good, and, second, we didn't have any money. The second problem seemed solvable. I got a job as a bartender to pay the rent and keep the lights on.

The place I tended bar turned out to be crucial: William's Pub, in the Uptown neighborhood of Minneapolis. It was a comedy club. I met dozens of young stand-up comics. I learned how to craft jokes and started writing some of my own. Among the people I befriended was a young comic, Tom Arnold, who also worked at William's. We became fast friends, and wrote together and did comedy bits together and were having the time of our lives until Marina became pregnant.

Okay, I thought, now it's really time to get a real job. My experience launching the magazine helped me land a job with a trade magazine publishing company that specialized in computer magazines. I left Minneapolis and took a job in their Peterborough, NH, offices. And that was apparently the end of my career in comedy. I spent the next eight years wearing a suit and being thoroughly respectable. I developed all sorts of useful skills such as how to do market research, how to create financial models on Excel, how to negotiate with vendors, and how to sell. I was so unhappy. And then one day in line at a supermarket I glanced at the tabloids and saw Tom Arnold on the cover with sitcom star Roseanne Barr!

I called him in Los Angeles. He immediately took my call and we talked and talked, and then he told me he wanted to hire me onto the "Roseanne" show but needed a writing sample. He sent me some scripts and asked me to write one of my own to see if I could do the job. Without a clue as to what I was doing, I wrote a script that must have been just good enough for him to justify hiring me. And so Marina, our five children, and I moved to Los Angeles. And voila! I had my dream job doing what I had dreamt of doing since I first saw Alan King telling jokes on the Ed Sullivan show nearly thirty years earlier.

But was it as good as I expected? Are you kidding me? Of course it was! I loved everything about writing for television. I loved sitting in the writing room with twelve other smart and funny people arguing all day about the script. I loved walking down to the stage and seeing our stuff in rehearsals, the taping nights in front of live studio audiences, and seeing great actors saying our jokes and getting laughs from the crowd. I loved the post-taping commiseration sessions at saloons near the studios and I loved the media acclaim.

And I was making great money. Writers/producers typically are paid on a per episode basis. At my level of experience and background in the late 90s, I made between $12,000 and $15,000 per episode for a 22 episode season. In addition, I had certain script guarantees. I received writing credit on at least three episodes per season, which paid another $20,000 per episode. A studio also paid me another $650,000 a year just to come up with ideas for television series. If one of my shows made it on the air and into syndication (endless reruns on afternoon local television), I could make tens, if not hundreds, of millions of dollars.

It was heaven. Except it wasn't for Marina. Or my family. The working hours were hideous: Most days started at 10 a.m. and ended at 3 a.m. The easy nights were the nights we filmed, when we finished by 10 p.m. I barely saw Marina and the children, except on weekends. Our house was not a home but the place I checked into when I wasn't working. Marina, meanwhile, struggled to deal with eight children. Both my family and my marriage started to fall apart. My comedy writer skillset — being a quick-witted wisenheimer who could debate endlessly — didn't transfer well to a home setting. Whereas I was well-compensated to have a dad in a sitcom make a joke out of his daughter's emotional crisis, it wasn't funny with real daughters and real sons and a real wife. It was irritating and provoked resentment.

So I had to make a change. I had to quit my dream job. (And honestly, I probably only had a few more working years left because comedy writers rarely work into their fifties.) I had carefully saved and we had lived well below our means, so I decided to take a couple of years off to devote time to my real job: husband and father.

For the next two years, I did that job full-time. We restored balance to our family life, and I was happy. I decided it was time to return to television.

Television, however, had other ideas. In the interim, reality programming had boomed. It made perfect economic sense: It was cheap to produce and audiences were interested. The number of sitcoms plummeted and so did employment for comedy writers. The fall primetime network schedule in 2002-03 had 43 sitcoms. When I returned in 2004-2005, there were 32. My agent told me there were about half as many jobs available as there were when I left.

By 2007-08, there were only 18 sitcoms on the air. I was now nearly 50 years old and had been out of the business for two years. Nobody was going to hire me anymore. My agent told me that I faced a common problem for writers my age: Producers could hire a team of first-time writers for less than the fee they would pay me for my services. But they won't know what they're doing, I countered. They don't care, he responded.

I had prudently saved and invested during my years in television, so I had a $500,000 nest egg between various mutual funds and an annuity I had invested in during my working years. But I was supporting a pretty large infrastructure.

The expensive part of having eight children isn't the present: feeding and clothing them. The expensive part of having eight children is their future. Good schooling was our priority. But there was no way we could send eight children to private schools, even with an enormous salary. We had to find a great public school system, and we did in San Marino, an old-money suburb near Los Angeles. In 1995, we bought a house there. It was a big one because, well, we needed a big one. And then there are all the other investments you make in their future: piano lessons, club sports fees, tutoring, and so on.

After a year, when it became clear that I could not return to television, I realized that I would have to pursue my old career: magazine publishing. I sent out hundreds of resumes. Nothing. With our savings running down over the next two years, we did what everyone advised in the mid 2000s: take advantage of the soaring equity in our house. We refinanced and refinanced and refinanced again, taking out money for living expenses each time. This was considered a smart move by many in those years.

But eventually we reached our limits. At one point, the water was shut off for several days when we failed to pay a bill. Under cover of darkness, we hooked up a hose to the outside spigot of our neighbor's house and ran the hose into our kitchen. We filled pots to cook pasta with and to heat up for sponge baths. It's amusing to think about now, but at the time it was mortifying. We were stealing water! From the nice old lady who lived next door!

Finally, in 2006, unable to refinance any further, we lost our home to foreclosure. Actually, you don't lose the house. The house loses you. The house isn't going anywhere. You and your family are the ones who get lost. In our case, an investor bought the house with the intention of renovating it and flipping it. I hope she made money on it.

The worst moment is the day the sheriff comes. Two armed members of the county sheriff's department showed up with a locksmith as we were moving out. The investor stood on the opposite side of the street as we packed and loaded a moving van. She watched us load our furniture, which we put into storage because the two bedroom apartment we managed to lease with the help of a friend didn't have room for 4,000 square feet worth of furniture. The deputies came and talked with us to make sure we really were moving out, and we felt like criminals for spending a final few hours in the house we owned for twelve years.

Over the next couple of years, our economic situation worsened. I couldn't find any kind of work. When I applied at Trader Joe's, the manager saw four years of unemployment and twelve years spent writing television comedy. Sir, are you sure you want stack loaves of bread here at Trader Joe's? Yes, I really do. Well, we've decided to hire the 24 year-old woman with purple hair and nose piercings instead.

The Writer's Guild of America has a term for my situation: They call it "The Gap." It's the time period between when your years as a working writer end and your retirement begins. I actually have an excellent pension for when I finally retire. The Guild is a strong union and it has negotiated an excellent pension plan for writers who have more than seven consecutive years of service. When I finally hit 65, my WGA pension combined with Social Security means I should have a comfortable retirement.

I was 46 when I had my last writing job in television. That meant I faced a 19 year Gap. As with other writers facing The Gap, my resume was a problem. I worked as a publishing executive before becoming a writer. I had a nice, solid resume that showed constant forward progress in my publishing career from financial analyst to business manager to circulation director. Which is great... except that progress ended in 1991 and I was applying in 2004.

I sent off resumes and scored occasional interviews. But the interviewers mainly wanted to hear Hollywood stories and then said, "Thanks we'll be in touch." I don't blame them. I'd hire the person currently working in the magazine business instead of the guy who had a lot of amusing stories about comedy writing but hadn't worked in a publishing environment for more than a decade.

By 2008, with the older children off at college or working and my job prospects bleak, Marina and I decided to separate. She moved to San Francisco with our two youngest daughters and settled in temporarily with two of our oldest daughters who worked there. I could no longer even afford to house myself. I found friends to take in my two remaining high schoolers.

And then I became homeless.

Yes, I, David Raether, the smart and funny guy who graduated with honors from college and read thousands of books and played the piano and went to church and won television awards, was homeless.

What happens when you hit bottom? I can tell you one thing: you don't bounce back. You crawl back, fighting every step of the way. It isn't a straight arc back up either; there are dozens of setbacks every step of the way. And the place you land isn't anywhere near where you were when you slipped off the cliff.

In the first days and weeks after I became homeless, I was in a daze, utterly and completely disoriented. I felt like a boxer staggering around the ring after a rapid series of blows I didn't see coming. It took me several months to figure it all out.

When you become homeless, you face a number of practical issues. In fact, when you are homeless, all you face are practical issues.

Where am I going to sleep tonight? What supermarket has the best samples today with the most protein in them? How am I going to deal with rainstorms dumping water into my usual sleeping spot? I have a job interview; I have clean clothes, but how can I make sure I don't smell? These are the issues you deal with on a daily basis. Dreary, boring, painful issues that relate directly to your body. And that's because homelessness is a dreary, boring, and often painful condition.

Your days are very long. The rhythm of work followed by home is gone. It's replaced by long stretches of empty time. No company, no conversation, no deadlines, nothing.

Several years earlier, one of my sons played on a mainly Hispanic soccer team in Bell Gardens, a working class Hispanic suburb of Los Angeles. I got to know one of the fathers quite well. He was from Guatemala City.

> *"What's Guatemala City like?"* I asked him one day.

> *"The days are very long in Guatemala City,"* he said.

That was all he said about his life there. And that would probably be the best description of life as a homeless person. The days are very long.

In my past life, I spent a typical autumn Saturday reading the paper and drinking several pots of coffee while working two or three crossword puzzles. Around 11 a.m., Marina and I would drive one or two or six of the kids to the farmers' market in the parking lot at Pasadena High School. Then we would return home and I would come up with an interesting set of reasons for not working in the yard while settling down on the couch to watch college football. Several hours later, I'd pour a glass or two of wine as the day turned into night, watch a movie, and settle into bed. Not much of a day, really. But when I think of those days now, they seem like some kind of lost paradise.

***

A Saturday during my homelessness went like this.

I would wake up around 4 a.m., brush myself off, and wander around the streets for awhile until Starbucks opened. I'd spend what little money I had on coffee and hope someone left a copy of *The Los Angeles Times* so I could work the crossword puzzle. I'd wait. And wait. At 10 a.m., the Pasadena Central Library opens. I would walk up there and surf job websites and send off some resumes and read articles online during my allotted time until noon, or, if I was lucky, early afternoon.

That was the hard part of the day. I'd be hungry. Really hungry. A week since I had a real meal hungry. I'd walk over to Whole Foods on the Arroyo Parkway, which has good food samples on Saturdays, grab a cart, and pretend to shop. (It always helps to put some items in the cart to look the part.) The fruits are by the door — I'd grab a bunch of orange slices and watermelon chunks. Next I go upstairs to where the muffin bits and cheese chunks are and gorge as subtly as possible. I'd return the unpurchased items to their places in the store and exit.

By then it would be mid-afternoon. I'd dream of lying on a couch in a warm living room, watching college football. Instead I would walk to another public library to access the Internet. As the sun sets, I'd head to a coffeehouse in South Pasadena called Kaldi where I could find someone to talk with. It wasn't the company of loved ones, but they were decent people who didn't ask too many questions about my circumstances

Night. At 8 p.m. I'd return to the Starbucks. I would find discarded copies of *The New York Times* and start working the crossword puzzle. And that was Saturday.

Sundays were the same, and so were Monday and Tuesday and Wednesday and Thursday and Friday. On public holidays, the libraries closed and I needed to find someplace else to spend my days. Only the rare job interview broke the monotony.

Gradually, however, I adjusted. I accepted that I was not going to have a career anytime soon, but I did need a job. I was not going to own a house, but I did need to find a place to live. I couldn't cook or afford restaurants, but I did need to eat.

After the first few disorienting weeks of homelessness, I got myself up off the canvas and begin to bob and weave and shake my head. I sniffed the ammonia capsule of reality and realized that I was in the biggest battle of my life.

During the nearly 18 months I spent homeless off and on, and during the ensuing years, I learned that I am more resourceful than I ever imagined, less respectable than I ever figured, and, ultimately, braver and more resilient than I ever dreamed. An important tool in my return to life has been Craigslist. It was through Craigslist that I found odd jobs — gigs, they often are called — doing everything from ghost-writing a memoir for a retired Caltech professor who had aphasia to web content writing jobs to actual real jobs with actual real startups.

Real companies advertise career jobs on Craigslist, but gigs were a godsend because they didn't require five years of similar professional work, recent recommendations, or even a permanent residence. Pay generally ran between $10 to $15 per hour.

The ghost-writing work was the perfect example of a

Craigslist gig. I ghost-wrote for a professor in his eighties. He had lived a remarkable life: traveling all over the world, writing dozens of books, and becoming a respected figure in academia. In his late eighties, however, he suffered a stroke as he began to write his memoirs. The stroke afflicted him with aphasia, which basically is an inability to communicate. He couldn't put together more than a few words at a time, couldn't type, and couldn't write. But his mind was still sharp and he could read and edit.

So I sat in his office and took notes as he haltingly described an incident or person he wanted to write about. I would guess at what he was trying to tell me and if I was right, he'd say yes. And then I'd try to re-narrate the story back to him to verify it. It was painstaking work, but after two years of occasional afternoons in his office, we produced a book. He died not long after that, and the book was never published.

I worked a number of other gigs: I provided editorial content for a commercial real estate agent's website, helped high school seniors write college essays, worked as an office equipment mover, and helped re-organize a small warehouse.

I got my first Craigslist gig in early 2009. When I managed to string together a couple of these at the same time, I could save enough money to rent a room for around $500 a month. Craigslist advertises a nearly endless supply of rooms available for rent. The situation is always the same: Hey, we have a roommate who is traveling/away for the semester/in rehab or jail and we need to rent out a room in our apartment to help pay the rent. You don't need a credit report, three references, and a deposit. All you need, usually, is to show up, look clean, and be willing to move out when the regular tenant returns from Europe/rehab/jail. I was able to rent a room by late winter of 2009 after seven months of homelessness. But I was homeless again by summer until I managed to save enough to rent a room once again in the fall.

These situations can be quite nice, and not too many questions are asked. I once lived in a house owned by a young Pasadena attorney who was on a two-month assignment in New York and needed someone to house sit. Some, however, can be dicey. I came home one day to a ramshackle house in northeast Pasadena and there was a gun on the kitchen counter. I moved out a couple days later. I have an intrinsic objection to handguns; I just didn't want to live in a place where the other residents were better armed than I was.

Losing my career and home changed my economic circumstances and day to day life. But it also upended my priorities. At the peak of my career, I ferociously pursued my goal of creating a hit TV show. It was my greatest ambition — and a lucrative one. But after years of homelessness and isolation, my single greatest desire became company. I wanted to spend more and more time with family and the people I loved. The goal of having a hit television show in syndication seemed so uninteresting compared to sitting across the table from my two daughters in a small apartment that we shared. Family and love became my top priorities. Everything else seemed insignificant. I had lost everything else, but these were still my children and I missed them and they missed me.

This desire led me to one of the most remarkable services on Craigslist: Rideshare. Rideshare is a refined form of hitchhiking. Let's say you want to go from Los Angeles to San Francisco to visit your daughters. On the Rideshare listings you can find someone making that drive who is looking for a rider to pitch in for gas and help with the driving. Or you can post your own ad: "I'm in Pasadena and want to go to Berkeley on Saturday. Flexible on time."

I traveled between Los Angeles and San Francisco a

hundred times and never had a problem. The car could be a bit crowded and the company a bit irritating, but most of the time I met interesting people: engineers, scientists, medical students, writers, artists, gallery owners, and guys like me — traveling to see their families on a budget. Most Rideshares I took cost about $35, which allowed me to see my now separated family far more than I would have otherwise.

In the years since I became homeless, Marina and I split up permanently. As a child, her parents had emigrated from Serbia to Germany, so she holds German citizenship. All of our children do as well. Germany has a stronger social safety net, so she decided to return with our two youngest daughters. They spent their high school years there and received a great education.

They are now fluent in German, but will return to the U.S. for college. I managed to find friends to host my children already in high school, so they could continue attending the same San Marino school. One of my daughters stayed mostly with one family, but one of my sons lived in fourteen different homes. Still, they graduated from one of the most elite public high schools in California, which prepared them for college. I remained active in their lives by visiting them after school each day, volunteering for school activities, and disguising my homelessness with my "San Marino disguise." It is a community of professionals: doctors, lawyers, and bankers. So whenever I met my children in a public place, I wore dress slacks, a dress shirt, and a tie. Friends and parents didn't need to know I was sleeping in parking garages.

The other children have finished college or are nearing completion. Two of them intend to go on to graduate school in the sciences. The rest have decent, solid careers in decent, solid professions such as business administration, nursing, and education. They are all funny and smart and not one of them has expressed an ounce of interest in becoming a television writer. Marina is happy and content in Germany, having fallen in love again there with a pleasant and quiet man.

I now live in Berkeley and have worked for several startups in the Bay Area as a content specialist. I currently blog for Degreed.com, a lifelong learning and self-education website in San Francisco. It keeps the wolf from the door, which is good because it means I actually have a door. I share a cozy house in Berkeley with two housemates.

My economic situation is still unstable; occasionally, I'll fall behind on rent. But it happens less frequently now and I've figured out enough about how to survive that I can recover from small setbacks like that. Since I moved to the Bay Area, I've worked at two startups. I had a substantial equity stake in one of them and was promised an equity stake in the other once the next round of financing came through. As I worked on them, I imagined having a full-time job, nice apartment, and good salary until retirement.

But neither panned out. I could despair when the startups fail or I fall behind on rent once again, but I just don't worry about stuff like that anymore. I already know what the worst possible outcome would be — homelessness — and I know I can survive that. So why ruin your day fretting about rent? I'll figure something out. I know how to take a punch and still keep standing.

So full-time, permanent employment in a real company with actual revenues is still an elusive prey. Life is still perilous for me and blogging is hardly a lucrative profession. But life is good. My emotional, psychological, and spiritual situation is considerably improved. I am close to my children, and I speak to most of them almost every day. I am healthy, strong, and full of hope and ambition again. I have survived failure. I lost my career, my home, all my savings — just about everything that seemed important. But I have held onto what I value much more: my children and their enduring love and affection, my health, and my ambition and self-belief.

And in the end, those were the only things worth keeping.

17.

HOW WE TREAT PETS
IN AMERICA

The American pet industry is almost as large as Americans' love for dogs and cats. In 2011, Americans spent nearly $51 billion on their 86.4 million cats and 78.2 million dogs. Our love affair with cats and dogs has produced luxury pet spas, home-cooked doggie meals, and Christmas cards that feature the family dog. More households have pets than have children.

Yet American shelters exterminate three to four million dogs and cats each year. Whether strays, abandoned pets, or the unwanted runt of a litter, they are killed by lethal injection. Our relationship with pets seems an odd juxtaposition of compassion and cruelty.

So where do all these pets come from? Who profits from breeding them? And why do we keep killing them? Answering these questions reveals that Americans' relationship with pets is less unique than one might expect; pet owners have treated animals like family members for generations, while tolerating or even accepting their mistreatment outside the home. Yet it also offers positive news for pet lovers: over the past four decades, the extermination and mistreatment of dogs and cats has steadily decreased.

A Dangerous Shelter

The number of stray cats and dogs in the United States is simply enormous. The American Society for the Prevention of Cruelty to Animals estimates that there are as many 70 million stray cats. A conservative estimate of 80 million stray cats and dogs would mean that the stray population is equal to one quarter of America's human population.

Animal shelters — the modern, more humane equivalent of dog pounds — strive to care for animals. They return lost pets to their owners and rehabilitate dogs and cats picked up by animal control for adoption. To find them good homes, many perform background checks or even make stringent demands on owners: a fenced in backyard, an understanding of pet ownership, and a commitment to obedience training and being home during the day. In the U.S., half of the pets that move through shelters every year find homes.

The other half, however, are killed. Given the large stray population, shelters are really in the business of population management. In all but a few European countries, shelters kill animals that are not claimed by an owner or adopted within a set amount of time, which is often less than a month. Since shelters do not re-release animals for public safety reasons, euthanization is the only way to avoid overfilling the shelter. Some shelters are "no-kill", but they are generally private shelters that have additional resources and less responsibility for the constant arrival of new animals. At any given time, approximately six to eight million pets are in a shelter, so three to four million dogs and cats are put down each year.

Yet Americans could drive than number down to near zero. While shelters struggle to manage eight million animals each year, Americans keep approximately 165 million dogs and cats as pets, and seventeen million Americans acquire a pet each year. Only 17% of pets are acquired from a shelter or rescue organization, and an additional 14%, especially cats, come from the stray population. Americans could easily adopt every animal up for adoption in a shelter. So why do we still kill so many pets each year?

An Invasive Species

While the stray population in the United States is enormous, the streets of American towns and cities are unusually free of stray dogs and cats, which are quite literally invasive species. In countries without resources devoted to managing strays, the number of stray dogs and cats on street corners is seemingly limitless.

As a result, veterinarians and pet advocacy groups recommend that people spay or neuter dogs and cats to combat overpopulation. Shelters, rescue organizations, and breeders seen as "responsible" all do, and this is often mandated by local law.

Many pet stores, breeders, and private owners do not, so many pets will have large litters of puppies or kittens. This remains the most common source of American pets, as some 42% of Americans get their pets informally from an acquaintance. For some animal advocates, this is a point of contention. This crowds out the market for rescued and stray pets, indirectly contributing to high euthanization rates. Every puppy sold or given away, the argument goes, makes it more likely that one in a shelter will be put to death.

But the focus on overpopulation can also obfuscate the cause of euthanizations. Of the pets received by shelters, 30% to 50% come from owners relinquishing their pets. The most common reasons cited by owners leaving their pets? They were moving, the landlord did not allow the pet, they had too many animals, or they could not afford the cost of food and veterinary care. Regardless of the reason, when an owner gives up a pet to a shelter, it's a coin flip whether it will end up dead or with a new family.

The All-American Dog

The other reason Americans don't adopt the full slate of shelter animals, of course, is that most people dream of a golden retriever puppy — not a five year-old mutt from a shelter. Twenty two percent of American pets are purchased from pet stores or commercial breeders, which is more than the percentage adopted from shelters.

When Thornstein Veblen coined the term "objects of conspicuous consumption," he had in mind purebred dogs. According to Mark Derr, author of A Dog's History of America, purebreds began to be bred as "an extravagance for the wealthy" beginning in the late 18th century. In countries like China, rising middle classes ignore street dogs to mimic Westerners by buying from expensive breeders. In the U.S., people ignore even rescue organizations devoted to purebred dogs to pay thousands of dollars for purebred puppies.

The desire for puppies and purebreds — we focus on dogs, since the large number of stray cats means that the dog breeding industry is relatively larger — is met at the top of the market by the breeders of a small number of purebreds. Although some animal welfare advocates criticize buying a dog while so many unwanted pets are euthanized, others recommend these breeders. The high premium placed on purebreds allows them to raise dogs in idyllic conditions on sunny farms. They also maintain an ethos of professionalism and concern for their animals' welfare; they specialize in one breed, work to maintain its purity, spay and neuter most purchased animals, and screen their customers to vet out irresponsible pet owners.

But the obsession with purebreds can go too far. The inbreeding done to select certain characteristics for dogs, as well as the highly exaggerated features of some breeds, can result in genetic and medical problems. They range from mild — the popular labrador breed almost invariably suffers from eye and knee problems — to extreme: the bulldog's large head, flat face, and wrinkled snout leave it unable to mate or give birth without a caesarian section, and they can barely breathe and exercise. One study on the problems bulldogs face concluded, "Many would question whether the breed's quality of life is so compromised that its breeding should be banned."

The Pet Factories

The vast majority of animals, however, are not bred in utopian pastures. They come from large-scale commercial breeders: anywhere from 2,000 to 10,000 American businesses that produce approximately two million animals a year, mostly dogs.

Although the United States is already overpopulated with dogs and cats, dog breeding operations can earn six-figure profits. The average female breeding dog can produce 9.4 puppies per year. A large breeder may have 100 female dogs and sell puppies for $500 each wholesale or more retail. That operation will make almost half a million dollars in revenue per year with each dog generating approximately $4,700.

This revenue, however, could easily be eaten up by the costs of pet care. These businesses can only profit by minimizing their expenditures on the animals they use for breeding. This often results in conditions on par with factories that mass produce chickens and pigs for slaughter, and it leads critics to call these breeding operations "puppy mills."

A number of rescue organizations have raided these mills, and the accounts would shock any pet owner: stacks of wire cages and crates crowded with dogs, rescuers in gas masks handling scared animals, and sick dogs with matted hair, skinny bodies, and glazed eyes. When dogs used for breeding get to an age where they are no longer needed, they are killed. Some puppy mills will call rescue organizations to pick up a dog they would otherwise kill, and it often takes a year for the dog to overcome its anxiety and enjoy human touch.

Raids take place on the basis of compelling evidence of animal cruelty. But the average puppy mill is not actually illegal. One minimum standard under the Animal Welfare Act, the sole federal law regulating these breeders, only requires that an animal be kept in a cage six inches longer than its body in any direction — even if it is never allowed out of its cage.

As a result, some three thousand puppy mills, which only meet minimum standards like these, are certified and inspected by the U.S. Department of Agriculture. Internal audits of the USDA have consistently found that it fails to enforce even these meager standards. In an extreme example, inspectors found dogs that resorted to cannibalism, but did not immediately revoke the breeder's license. Other serious violations resulted only in warning after warning. Meanwhile, major breeders selling directly to the public, rather than through another seller like a pet store, are not subject to any federal law, and often to no state law.

In the absence of legal standards, conditions in puppy mills fall to the lowest common denominator; breeders simply view dogs differently than pet owners. The breeders come together to swap dogs at auctions throughout the Midwest, where they reveal a perspective of viewing animals dispassionately as tools. In typical exchanges, filmed by animal welfare activists, an auctioneer asks his audience, "Where else you gonna find something to produce you over $2,000 gross in a year?" and reminded everyone that the dogs, "Got their whole lives in front of 'em to work for ya."

As a result, pet advocates assert, almost any puppy bought from a pet store or online (or from any breeder that does not insist on a site visit to see the puppy with its parents) came from a puppy mill. These breeders sell millions of dogs per year, and by selling dogs through brokers, pet stores, or online, breeders can sell puppies without customers ever being wise to the plight of the puppies' parents. One exposé, which gained prominence when featured on Oprah, showed viewers adorable puppies playing in a pet store, then tracked down their parents to squalid conditions like those described above.

A rare study on pet shops and puppy mills in California found that 44% of those visited had sick or neglected animals" and 25% "did not have adequate food or water." Animal welfare groups believe that in states like Pennsylvania and Missouri, which have fewer legal protections and less consumer awareness, yet are home to most large-scale dog breeding operations, those numbers are much worse.

A Cash Crop

The current condition of America's dogs and cats — valued and treated as part of the family, but also valued and treated like a commodity — is neither new nor novel. In the West, pets have faced this seemingly contradictory situation for some two hundred years.

In Europe, many dogs escaped their kennels and breached their owners' homes centuries ago. Mary Todd Lincoln, when asked about her husband's hobbies, described them as follows: "cats." After the Civil War, as urbanization began to rapidly move Americans off farms and into cities, selling pets became an industry serving the middle class. Attitudes toward pets followed a "Victorian ethic" by which compassion for animals was seen as civilized and cruelty as "one outward expression of inward moral collapse."

We might assume that today's pet owners, who lavish as much attention on pets as their own children, are the height of pet adoration. But the 1800s saw devotion every bit as maniacal.

In *Pets in America: A History*, Katherine C. Grier recounts the following story:

> *The most inspired pet-keeping was surely practiced by the Rankin children of late 19th-century Albany, who turned a hutchful of rabbits "rescued from their fate as someone's dinner" into a carefully documented kingdom that was reorganized as a republic, complete with a declaration of independence, a census, a postal system and taxes. Over the years, the Bunnie States of America spun off a map company and a medical college.*

This co-existed, however, with inhumane treatment for animals not kept as pets. The phrase "dog days of summer" took on new meaning as city-dwellers systematically hunted down dogs in return for bounties to prevent the spread of rabies. Manhattan's stray dogs were caught, locked in a cage, and lowered into the East River to be drowned on a daily basis. Americans generally justified this cruelty as part of the "natural order." Man had dominion over animals, and could treat them as he saw fit. The majority of Americans, even pet owners, saw no reason to afford any protections to a stray or working animal.

The first puppy mills arose after World War II. The

U.S. Department of Agriculture encouraged farmers to breed puppies as a new "cash crop" for the burgeoning pet store market. No oversight or laws existed on the practice. Unsurprisingly, farmers that had been devastated by the Great Depression, survived World War II, and used animals as tools did not prioritize the comfort of the dogs. They remained locked inside refashioned chicken coops, without access to veterinary care or "socialization" with humans and other dogs.

While puppy mills had poor conditions, the view of dogs as a commodity meant that they were euthanized and discarded in large numbers. In the words of one president of a New England animal shelter:

> *"In the past, it was acceptable to throw an animal away, the way you would an old television set. You would just bring them to the shelter and dump the old dog you don't want anymore... For a long time, it's just what you did. [Animals] came in; you killed them. No one thought that was wrong"*

Pet owners felt no qualms over abandoning unwanted dogs, while pet stores dropped off puppies that grew too old to sell and breeders discarded old animals. By 1970, overcrowded shelters euthanized over 20 million animals.

Four Decades of Change

In 2011, the number of animals euthanized stood at approximately three million — an incredible decrease from the 20 million mark in 1970, especially considering that the number of pets, according to the American Society for the Prevention of Cruelty to Animals, has doubled from 80 million dogs and cats to 160 million.

The movement to spay and neuter dogs and cats began in 1971 when a Los Angeles shelter opened a low-cost spay/neuter clinic. It framed sterilization as an issue of compassion. In its first four years, spaying and neutering increased from 10% to 51% in Los Angeles among licensed dogs. Crucially, the clinic and its followers not only spread spaying and neutering as a norm (both among shelters and through outreach programs), but also subsidized the cost of the procedure — a crucial point for low-income pet owners as sterilization costs several hundred dollars.

States and local government also began mandating the practice of spaying and neutering. The laws are not uniform, but 30 states have some form of spay/neuter laws. As a result, 78% of pet dogs are now spayed or neutered, and sterilization is considered, in the words of Inga Fricke of the United States Humane Society, "a standard practice of care."

The improving lot of pets can also be linked to the establishment of responsible pet care as a norm. Whereas pets were once a commodity or tool, a myriad of organizations now publish manuals that sternly lecture owners on the responsibilities that come with the "privilege" of pet ownership. Online searches on "where to buy a puppy" return hundreds of articles on the evils of puppy mills and retail pet stores. Anyone posting to an email list or online forum asking where to give up their pet can expect to face a horde of self-righteous, finger-wagging pet advocates.

With increased care for the welfare of pets came increased resources to improve their treatment. The amount shelters spent on animal protection increased from roughly $1 billion to $2.8 billion from 1975 to 2007, accounting for inflation. Rescue and advocacy organizations have proliferated. Petfinder, a database of adoptable pets, offers links to nearly 14,000 adoption groups.

Increased legal attention has focused on puppy mills in addition to spaying, neutering, and animal cruelty. Many local governments have placed more stringent conditions on dog breeding than the federal minimum, and a number of cities have banned the sale of dogs and cats in pet stores outright to prevent the sale of puppy mill pups: LA became the biggest city to do so in 2012, joining 27 other major cities.

The past four decades have seen dramatic improvement in the lot of America's pets. Euthanization has fallen dramatically thanks to legal action, increased resources, and the norms of responsible pet care, which have also taken aim at puppy mills and animal cruelty.

The recession has, however, reversed some of these gains. When we visited the San Francisco Department of Animal Care, which is mandated to accept any dog in San Francisco for any reason, employees described a significant increase in the number of dogs dropped off by owners who could not afford to buy food for their dog or pay for veterinary care, as well as people who tried (and failed) to make cash by breeding chihuahua and pitbull puppies.

A Dog's Life

America's relationship with pets is a mixed bag. People clearly love their pets; we also kill millions of them each year. But the number of pet euthanizations keeps dropping as more pets are sterilized, more people adopt, and fewer people treat pets like commodities. If 1970 marked the high-water mark in pet cruelty, massive strides have been made since then.

But focusing only on euthanizations misses part of the story. Hidden behind a cloak of respectability, pet stores and brokers continue to sell puppies that came from exploitive "puppy mills." Pet-loving Americans are mostly ignorant of the plight of the cute, cuddly creatures that they love to croon over. Americans don't know much about the factories where their phones, shoes, and computers come from. Perhaps it's not surprising that the same is true of our beloved pets.

18.

EVICTED IN SAN FRANCSICO

In March of 2014, 75-year old Inge Dhillion was evicted from her San Francisco residence; her possessions were forcibly moved into a storage unit, and she was left without a home. She now sleeps in a brown 1997 Volvo station wagon with her cat, Queenie, parked in front of her old home in the Mission District. She steals ice from motel machines to chill her daily insulin shots, and relies on the goodwill of social workers to help her through daily life.

Within a few weeks of the eviction, the landlord put the property on the market for $1.4 million; it's a good time to sell, considering he bought the place for $627,000 in 2002.

What follows is the story of one eviction in San Francisco, as recounted by both Inge and her landlord.

A Free Spirit

Inge Dhillon was 24 years old when she snuck on a cargo ship in Rotterdam and embarked on a 10-day journey bound for the United States. She'd fallen in love with a beautiful woman, and decided to go find her in Philadelphia.

She grew up in post-war Germany, working odd jobs to get by: delivering flowers to prostitutes, hostessing on a first class train across the countryside, butchering hogs in dingy back rooms. With the promise of a better life, she had set her sails to the sea.

When she arrived, the Philadelphia love affair didn't pan out — her mistress had "gone straight" — and Inge made a second impulsive decision: she'd embark for San Francisco to find the "dyke that dreams are made of." When she arrived, she recalls being popular with the ladies — "I was passed around like wildfire!" — but also remembers a fairly hostile recognition by the police as a gay woman in the 1960s:

> *"I used to go to this little bar somewhere on Harrison Street. It'd be packed with women, and the police would operate these 'queer raids.' You'd hear a blaring noise, and the warning light would flood the room. They'd round up the broads and throw them in the paddy-wagon."*

She joined the International Brotherhood of the Teamsters and drove a Yellow Cab around the city for the next 27 years, holing up in a variety of rooms and apartments. In 1994, she settled in an illegal in-law unit on Rosemont Street: she'd call this home for 20 years.

Her living space was quaint: A 350 square foot illegal in-law unit attached to a garage, with a small kitchen and a half-bath. For a retired taxi driver trying to cut it in a tough San Francisco housing market, a $480 monthly rent was hard to beat.

Illegal In-Law Units in SF: A Brief Note

An in-law unit is a small additional dwelling to a main property. There are three stipulations that may make an in-law unit illegal in San Francisco: no separate PG&E bill (gas and electric bill is shared with or paid by landlord); ceiling height is lower than 7'6"; and, most commonly, the unit has no independent front entrance, or secondary egress (for example, a unit where the only entrance/exit is through a garage).

Usually, illegal units exhibit at least two of these tendencies; in Inge's case, her unit exhibited all three. She paid no gas or electricity bill, lived in a unit below mandated size, and had to enter and exit through the main unit's garage.

City officials estimate that there are over 40,000 illegal in-law units attached to San Francisco properties, and they account for about ten percent of the city's housing stock. Most of these units were constructed during World War II, when workers flooded to the Bay Area to take wartime industrial jobs; today, property owners often choose to rent them to lower-income tenants under the table. Historically, San Francisco has had a "don't ask, don't tell" policy regarding illegal in-law units; when they are reported, the city takes serious action.

Leading up to Inge's Eviction

Inge began renting the illegal unit on Rosemont Street in 1994, from "an old German man" who'd owned the property for years and was willing to help out a fellow national. When the current owners, the Withrington brothers, purchased the property in 2002, Inge came with it.

In San Francisco, a landlord can't evict a current tenant just because they are selling or buying the property; by the time the unit was purchased, Inge had already been living there for ten years, and she had no intention to go anywhere. Since Inge's unit was illegal, her landlord had even fewer options in the way of legal recourse.

"Pretty much everyone we talked to advised us not to buy it," says Jon Withrington, with a defeated chuckle. "We probably should've listened." What ensued was a drawn-out sticky situation that pitted him against his senior citizen tenant.

At first, Withrington accepted Inge's presence; her unit was fairly disconnected from the main two-story unit. He and his brother, who had co-invested in the property, each occupied a floor with their respective families. But over time, he came to realize that Inge was a destructive tenant and "came across as a victim, but was her own worst enemy":

> *"I could send you transcripts of a phone message where she said she will burn the house down if we didn't fix the leaking roof. Or show you the rent increase letter that was returned to me unopened and defaced with 'Fuck You' written on it. We tried to help her."*

He also claims that Inge made enemies with many neighbors over trite things like "turning the sprinklers on near her cat." In December 2011, one of these conflicts led to an anonymous report filed with San Francisco's Department of Building Inspection (DBI), in which someone "ratted on" Inge's illegal unit. Since the claim was completely anonymous, it technically could've been made by anyone — including the landlord.

In the following weeks, the DBI contacted Wingrington, told him the nature of the complaint, and conducted an inspection of the property, deeming that the unit was illegal. The DBI offered the landlord a choice: he could either retrofit the in-law unit to make it legal (this would require him to rip out the garage and extend an independent entrance, at a cost of around $150,000), or he could remove the unit (this would entail converting the unit into a workshop at a cost of about $4,000). He chose the latter.

But in order to convert the unit into a workshop, Wingrington would have to do two things: acquire the necessary permits to do so, and then evict Inge.

He described the eviction process as "hellish." To convert the unit, he had to get electrical, plumbing, and building permits; he started with the building permit, but Inge — with the help of social workers and lawyers — appealed it. He took the matter to the Board of Appeals, but Inge made the compelling case that she was elderly, sick, and had nowhere to go; a hold was put on any construction work for three months, and Inge was ordered to make a concerted effort to find alternative housing.

***

In San Francisco, there exist a number of housing resources for seniors facing eviction. Openhouse, a housing service specifically for LGBT (lesbian, gay, bi/trans-sexual) seniors like Inge, helps community members find affordable housing by providing resources in weekly housing clinics and by setting them up with services for eviction defense, housing rights, employment, and mental health counseling. The program also plans to open a 110-unit apartment complex with rooms ranging from $589 to $1000 per month, or 30% of a tenant's income (usually social security, SSI, or disability pay).

The problem, according to Inge, is that most housing options like this have extremely long wait lists. Ellyn Bloomfield, Openhouse's social service manager, confirms this:

> *"On any given day in San Francisco, there are about 15,000 elderly looking to be placed in affordable housing. The average wait list time is five years; for many, this is just too long. They need something more immediately."*

Bloomfield, who was a gerontologist before going into social work, also says that eviction is a common dilemma faced by San Francisco's elderly. She adds that laws like the Ellis Act — which makes it legal for landlords to evict tenants as long as they don't rent the property for five years afterward — are especially painful for tenants to go through, and that landlords often single them out as high-maintenance roadblocks:

> *"Older people are forced into exile by their landlords, under a variety of eviction laws — almost like post-war refugees. Many actually even have post-traumatic stress disorder. What other business exists where there is an adversarial relationship between a client and a manager?"*

There are other options, like single room occupancies (SROs), which are often used to house the homeless community as well. But in San Francisco, the majority of these are in the Tenderloin (one of the city's most dangerous neighborhoods), and for an elderly woman, this isn't the safest environment.

According to Inge, she pursued some of these options, but was turned off by the no-guarantee nature of the wait-lists, and felt she was entitled to stay where she was. Withrington says the tenant was "in denial of the impending eviction," and, despite his efforts to set her up with resources, Inge did little in way of seriously considering outside options.

> *"I personally went out and found stuff — my own mother personally went out and found stuff. We put Inge in touch with multiple social workers and housing agencies. The problem is that a lot of these places come and check where you're living and only take you in if you meet their standards. Inge is a hoarder, a smoker, and has a cat. The smell in her unit was absolutely...just...unbelievable. That didn't work out well for her."*

Over the years, Inge's rent had gradually increased from $480 to $560 per month; in late 2012, in the midst of the permit debacle, she decided to stop paying rent altogether. Withrington says he "couldn't do a damn thing about it," since he was renting an illegal unit. In addition, Inge refused to contribute to gas, water, and electricity bills. Inge's landlord says that, in all, this cost him over $10,000 in utilities and lost potential rent.

The landlord was caught in a legislative catch-22: he faced immense fines from the DBI if he didn't remove the illegal unit, but the Board of Arbitration wouldn't grant him the necessary permits to do so. But removing the legal unit would also prove to be a loophole to legally evict Inge and pave the way for a more lucrative property sale (properties with 'squatters' don't sell for nearly as much).

In early 2013, after the three month stay on construction was up, Inge and Withrington were summoned back to the Board of Appeals; this time, Inge didn't even show up. By default, the landlord got the permit. To begin converting the illegal in-law unit into a legal workspace, he'd need to evict Inge.

The Eviction and Aftermath

Under Rent Ordinance section 37.9(a)(10), once a landlord has obtained the applicable permits to "demolish or otherwise remove the [illegal] rental unit from housing use," the tenant can be legally evicted. Armed with the necessary paperwork, Withrington began the eviction process but, according to him, Inge was still in denial of the process:

> *"I told her, okay look Inge, we're going to*
> *start this process now. Are you going to*
> *find a place to live? She essentially told me*
> *to [stick it where the sun doesn't shine]."*

First came the arbitration hearing, where Inge's lawyer and the landlord's lawyers tried to strike a deal to avoid any type of elongated legal dispute. This ended somewhat peacefully: Withrington agreed to pay Inge a settlement of $14,000 in resettlement fees, and she signed a contract agreeing to vacate the property within 60 days. The first eviction notice was issued.

The 60 days came and went, and Inge was still occupying the property. A second eviction notice, known as an "unlawful detainer," or the act of occupying property without legal right, was issued. This time, Inge had five days to appear before the Board of Appeals to argue her case. Again, she failed to show up.

Then it got ugly: a third eviction was issued — a "Sheriff's notice." The Sheriff posted a "notice to vacate," and gave Inge five days to leave; when she failed to, she was forcefully removed, and all of her belongings were taken out of her unit and placed in a storage unit. "It took three truck loads to get her stuff out," recalls Withrington. "And the help of a whole team of social workers."

With the unit successfully vacated, the landlord proceeded to convert it into a workshop. This consisted of ripping out the kitchen and converting the full bath into a half-bath, at a cost of $10,000, according to a building report filed with the DBI. In total, Withrington estimates he spent upwards of $40,000 on remodeling, lawyers' fees, permits, lost rent, and utilities.

Only a few months after the eviction, he listed the property for sale. Inge's once-illegal in-law unit was now advertised as a "legal work studio." After less than ten days of being on the market, an offer "considerably higher than the asking price" of $1.4 million was made. Though it would've been difficult to sell the property with Inge squatting in it, the landlord claims the sale was not premeditated and had nothing to do with the recent eviction:

> *"My brother, who was a co-investor and resident in the main property, had just had a baby with his wife, and they wanted to sell and find a more suitable place to raise a family."*

It's a Good Time to Be Bornstein & Bornstein

Throughout the eviction process, Withrington was represented by Daniel Bornstein, one half of the highly controversial Bornstein and Bornstein law office. For 20 years, Bornstein has been evicting tenants on behalf of landlords in San Francisco and has become the heralded leader in this space.

He even runs a free "Eviction Boot Camp," in which he rallies up disgruntled landlords and coaches them on how to appropriately (and legally) remove unwanted tenants. One client expresses why she prefers to use Bornstein in dire straights:

> *"If my gentle persuasion does not work,*
> *Daniel provides the big stick. An eviction is*
> *a failure, and he's brilliant. He can stand*
> *up and [claim] that we're going to be*
> *throwing someone out on the street."*

The lawyers' Yelp page overflows with positive reviews from landlords who've successfully ousted a variety of tenants — "rent controlled freeloaders," "illegal dwellers," and "asshole renters" alike. But the lawyers' ethics have come into question on multiple occasions; last month, Bornstein was fined $12,069 for "deceptively undermining the integrity for judicial proceedings" — a charge that "indicates gross professional misconduct."

But Withrington "wasn't thinking about ethics" at the time of the eviction — he just wanted the problem resolved, and when it comes to resolving tenant issues, Daniel Bornstein reigns supreme. The landlord recalls his impressions upon first meeting Bornstein:

> *"I thought, 'he's just a lawyer doing lawyer*
> *stuff.' It wasn't really until later, during*
> *the appeals process that I realized he was*
> *a detested character. The Board nearly*
> *dismissed me from the room just because I*
> *was associated with him. There's quite a*
> *lot of hatred for that man."*

Nonetheless, it's a good time to be a Bornstein in San Francisco: in the past year alone, Ellis Act evictions have risen 170%; since 1997, there have been 3,811, and that number is constantly rising. Fifteen years ago, evictions were, in general, reserved for extreme cases of tenant misconduct; today, they are commonplace, and are often used to the benefit of landlords in the high-demand housing market. Bornstein has been the man behind the curtain, orchestrating tenant removals with practised precision.

For his part in Inge's case, Bornstein charged the landlord $300 per hour; all said and done, his services came with a $10,000 bill.

Living in a Volvo With Queenie

And what became of Inge? Following the eviction, the landlord helped her relocate to a nearby hotel. "It was filthy," she recalls:

> *"There was no toilet paper, and they refused to resupply it; there was a smashed-in window in my room, and the draft was so cold, I had to bury myself in a sleeping bag to stay warm. It was cash only, and everything was shady and under-the-table. It was one of the few times in my life where I didn't feel safe."*

After a few nights, she couldn't bear to stay there any longer. She got into her Volvo station wagon, drove back to Rosemont Street, parked outside of her old unit, and spent the night in her car.

A look inside her Volvo is enough to curdle a stomach of steel: trash bags are piled high in the back seat, open packages of food topple into a litter box full of cat feces, door-sides are crammed full of half-smoked Pall

Malls and prescription painkillers.

Queenie, a seven-year-old cat Inge purchased through EBay classifieds, is relegated to the tiny foot space beneath the glove compartment. "She's a very strong-willed cat," Inge tells me from beneath her sleeping bag. "It took me about a year and a half to really bond with her. Now she's my best friend." Queenie survives on organic cat food donated by a "young hipster woman" who lives in the neighborhood.

Inge has an amalgam of health issues, the most serious of which is her high glucose levels. She has to take daily insulin shots, which must be chilled on ice.

> *"It's not the type of environment I can take my medications in. I have to keep the damn things chilled on ice, so that's a problem. Sometimes, a young lady down the street brings me ice. Other times, I have to go by Safeway or a hotel and raid an ice machine. I don't know how I'm surviving. I'm losing so much weight."*

Luckily, when Inge was a Teamster taxi driver all those years ago, she opted to take a pay cut to qualify for free health coverage through Kaiser; today, she still enjoys that benefit. In addition, she receives about $1,300 per month in disability and social security pay, and has "about $3,000 in quarter rolls" tucked away in a safe at her friend's apartment. But she claims this isn't enough to find a market-rate apartment that caters to her needs as a disabled elderly woman and cover her other expenses. Her settlement money comes in small increments, so it is difficult for her to save up.

She usually stays parked on or around Rosemont Street in the Mission District, and she receives street sweeping tickets on a weekly basis. She pays about $46 per month for her car insurance, and also pays $300 per month for the storage unit that has housed all of her belongings since the eviction, but she can't remember where it's located.

Occasionally, she'll splurge for a night at a the Civic Center Motel Inn, where she can capitalize on a free continental breakfast and clean herself up (when we met her, her nails were two inches long and black with grime from cleaning her cat's litter box). This runs her about $80 per night.

With an eviction on her record, Inge is convinced she won't be able to find a suitable place, but has social workers "begging away on computers" for her. We accompanied her to one resource center, Episcopal Community Services, where she was promptly told her only option was a homeless shelter for the night.

Her landlord's actions weren't intentionally maliious; Inge was by no means a perfect tenant, and even trended toward destructive at times. For years, the Withringtons cooperated with her, and they offered every resource they could during the eviction process: legal assistance, housing leads, and social service contacts. When we spoke with them, they were sympathetic and kind.

The Way Things Used to Be

Inge remembers the day she first moved into her place on Rosemont 20 years ago:

> *"I had just settled my things, and I was exhausted but very happy. I had this little record player, and I put on my favorite album. It was this little number by a Brazilian singer named Simone — she's a trip, I'm just nuts about her — called 'Bye Bye Brasil.'"*

She listened to the album for hours, flipping it from side to side, reflecting on life. "Of all the things I've got in that storage unit," she says, "the only thing I care about is my box of old records — the songs of escape, as I call them."

***

Since the eviction, Inge has been contemplating her own escape. Still a citizen of Germany, she has the option of repatriating to her homeland, which has a free program for nationals wishing to relocate. She'd be able to get off the plane, connect with social services, and get subsidized housing and medical coverage. But for 50 years, she has built a life for herself in San Francisco, and that's something she doesn't want to give up.

Inge drives from a social service center back to Rosemont Street, where she parks her car out in front of her old home. Queenie leaps up from the floor of the car, navigates through the mountain of trash on the passenger seat, and presses her paws against the window like a puppy.

"She remembers it," says Inge, "she wants to go dance in the garden."

19.

THE MCDONALD'S MONOPOLY FRAUD

The McDonald's Monopoly game is one of the most successful marketing promotions of all time. Every year, for a limited time only, customers can win big money collecting Monopoly pieces from the packaging of McDonald's products. Although the odds are in the same league as winning the Mega Millions lottery jackpot, someone who peels a Boardwalk off her medium soda and a Park Place off her cheeseburger will win $1 million. More often, customers win less lucrative prizes like a Filet-O-Fish.

The game has a cult following; even a number of people who despise fast food go to McDonald's each year to collect the pieces and take a shot at winning $1 million. The promotion is so successful that McDonald's has run it for over two decades. But from 1995 to 2001, the game had only one real winner: Jerome Jacobson, who cheated at McDonald's Monopoly to a tune of $20 million.

Careful Who You Let Be Banker

The key to a successful promotion like McDonald's Monopoly lies in the probabilities. Prizes need to be ubiquitous enough that the game is fun, but grand prizes need to be few and far between so that the bump in sales more than offsets the cost of the prizes.

Promotions usually achieve this by giving out lots of cheap prizes and only a handful of grand prizes. McDonald's Monopoly does the same by doling out sodas and medium fries to 1 in 4 instant winners, while some years no one finds the pieces necessary to win the $1 million grand prize.

The Monopoly setup, however, makes the odds behind grand prizes more deceiving. To win one, customers need to collect a full set of properties from the Monopoly game. An entire generation of parents has argued with children who demand McDonald's because they just need one more property to win. But everyone is just one game piece away from a grand prize. Rather than make each piece appear with the same probability, McDonald's makes one piece from each set extremely rare. So each year, thousands of people with 3 out of the 4 railroads are all searching for Short Line Railroad, with only 1 in 150 million odds of finding it.

The setup draws scammers, who put out Craigslist ads or post on forums that they have Park Place and want to team up with someone who has the extremely rare Boardwalk piece. Occasionally someone ignorant of the odds agrees; he or she sends the rare piece and never hears from the scammer again.

Jerome Jacobson had a simpler idea. Jacobson worked as head of security at Simon Marketing Inc., the company entrusted with running almost every McDonald's promotion from Happy Meal toys to the Monopoly game. Simon's internal policies called for 2 or 3 people to oversee the production and distribution of game pieces, but Jacobson alone oversaw the distribution of Monopoly pieces around the country. In 1989, two years into the running of the promotion, Jacobson stole a piece worth $25,000 and gave it to his stepbrother. By 1995, the former police officer was stealing all the pieces of value.

Fourteen years later, an article in the Florida Times-Union would reveal how Jacobson made off with the valuable real estate:

Jacobson oversaw a security process that began at a printing plant where pieces were made, separated by value and stored in a vault. He was responsible for transporting those pieces in sealed envelopes to plants that manufactured McDonald's food cartons and cups, where the pieces were supposed to be attached.

But Jacobson would slip into airport bathrooms, lock himself in stalls and carefully open the envelopes to steal the pieces. He received cash kickbacks for stealing 50 to 60 pieces and bought homes, cars and other property.

Jacobson couldn't redeem the pieces himself, nor could his family without attracting attention. Instead he sold the pieces to people he recruited through friends and family. Some of the recruits mortgaged their house to pay a mysterious figure they knew only as "Uncle Jerry." The prizes included $10,000 cash prizes, cars, and even the rare $1 million prize that McDonald's awarded with much fanfare.

In 1995, St. Jude Children's Hospital received an anonymous gift in the form of two McDonald's Monopoly pieces. A receptionist nearly threw the unmarked envelope away before discovering their value: the $1 million grand prize. Who was the anonymous donor behind this generous gift? Uncle Jerry of course.

Uncle Jerry Gets Caught

The scheme worked for six years, until someone recruited by Jacobson and his friends to win a 1996 Dodge Viper revealed the fraud to the FBI. The agency in turn launched "Operation Final Answer," in reference to Who Wants to Be a Millionaire, the television show that inspired another McDonald's promotion that Jacobson scammed.

The FBI informed McDonald's, but asked the fast food chain to continue running the contest so agents could collect evidence. Wiretaps, phone records, and (according to the FBI) "some of the most sophisticated and innovative investigative techniques available" helped the agency prove that the mysterious mastermind at the center of the scheme was Jerome Jacobson. The pattern of prize winners mortgaging their house just before they won provided evidence of Jacobson's scheme. Agents also followed several suspects as they met with recruiters, in one case going to, in the words of the FBI director, "a secluded lot in, of all places, Fair Play, South Carolina."

In court, Jacobson apologized for his actions. He earned $1 million himself from the fraud, which he returned as a result of the case. He was sentenced to 3 years in federal prison and was released on October 21, 2005. Some 51 other members of the conspiracy were indicted, and many pled guilty. Yet few faced stern sentences. On appeal, a Florida judge overturned the criminal sentences for four of the most central members of the plot.

McDonald's Monopoly Lives On

Uncle Jerry's actions didn't deter enthusiasm for the McDonald's Monopoly promotion.

McDonald's reacted to revelations of Jacobson's actions by going on damage control. It fired Simon Marketing Inc., taking its $500 million contract elsewhere, and announced an additional cash giveaway promotion worth $10 million in 55 cash prizes as an apology to players who for years had played a rigged game. (McDonald's did continue to pay St. Jude $50,000 installments on its million dollar prize, even though it was fraudulently won.) Most McDonald's customers kept playing the game, oblivious to the fact that Jacobson had rigged the game for years. The McDonald's Monopoly promotion is now over 25 years old.

Law enforcement and the media, meanwhile, had a hard time maintaining a serious tone during the investigation. Attorney General John Ashcroft stressed in an announcement that "We want those involved in this type of corruption to know that breaking the law is not a game." CNN's reporter deadpanned that "Jerome Jacobson allegedly monopolized McDonald's winning real estate." But the local Florida Times-Union probably said it best: "It's a scam only the Hamburglar could love."

20.

WHAT HAPPENS
TO STOLEN BICYCLES?

At Priceonomics, we are fascinated by stolen bicycles. Put simply, why the heck do so many bicycles get stolen? It seems like a crime with very limited financial upside for the thief, and yet bicycle theft is rampant in cities across the United States. What is the economic incentive for bike thieves that underpins the pervasiveness of bike theft? Is this actually an efficient way for criminals to make money?

It seems as if stealing bikes shouldn't be a lucrative form of criminal activity. Used bikes aren't particularly liquid or in demand compared to other things one could steal (phones, electronics, drugs, etc). And yet, bikes continue to get stolen, so they must be generating sufficient income for thieves. What happens to these stolen bikes, and how do they get turned into criminal income?

The Depth of the Problem

In San Francisco (where Priceonomics is located), if you ever leave your bike unlocked, it will be stolen. If you use a cable lock to secure your bike, it will be stolen at some point. Unless you lock your bike with medieval-esque u-locks, your bike will be stolen from the streets of most American cities. Even if you take these strong precautions, your bike may still get stolen.

According the National Bike Registry and FBI, $350 million in bicycles are stolen in the United States each year. Beyond the financial cost of the crime, it's heartbreaking to find out someone stole your bike; bikers love their bikes.

As one mom wrote in an open letter to the thief who pinched her twelve year old son's bike:

> *"It took CJ three weeks to finally decide on his bike. We looked at a brown bike at Costco, even brought it home to return it the next day, and a blue one at Target. But his heart was set on the green and black Trek he saw at Libertyville Cyclery. CJ knew it was more than we wanted to spend but the boy had never asked for anything before. You see, CJ had to live through his dad being unemployed for 18 months and knew money was tight. Besides, he's just an all around thoughtful kid.*
>
> *CJ didn't ride his bike to school if there was rain in the forecast and he always locked it up. You probably noticed that it doesn't have a scratch on it. CJ treated his bike really well and always used the kickstand.*
>
> *You should know that CJ has cried about the bike and is still very sad. He had to learn a life lesson a little earlier than I had*

> *liked - that there are some people in the*
> *world who are just plain mean. Now you*
> *know a little about my really awesome son*
> *and the story behind his green and black*
> *Trek 3500, 16-inch mountain bike."*

An Economic Theory of Bike Crime

In 1968, Chicago economist Gary Becker introduced the notion that criminal behavior could be modeled using conventional economic theories. Criminals were just rational actors engaged in a careful cost-benefit analysis of whether to commit a crime. Is the potential revenue from the crime greater than the probability adjusted weight of getting caught? Or, as the antagonist in the movie *The Girl Next Door* puts it, "Is the juice worth the squeeze?"

Criminal activity (especially crime with a clear economic incentive like theft) could therefore be modeled like any financial decision on a risk reward curve. If you are going to take a big criminal risk, you need to expect a large financial reward. Crimes that generate more reward than the probability weighted cost of getting caught create expected value for the criminal. Criminals try to find "free lunches" where they can generate revenue with little risk. The government should respond by increasing the penalty for that activity so that the market equilibrates and there is an "optimal" amount of crime.

For some thefts, the consequences of getting caught are quite severe. If you steal a person (kidnapping), you're risking going away to jail for a very long time. If you rob a bank, ditto. Even stealing a car is a felony that can result in jail time. Each of these crimes has a sufficiently high "risk" to at least somewhat counterbalance the "reward."

Risk Return Tradeoff of Crime

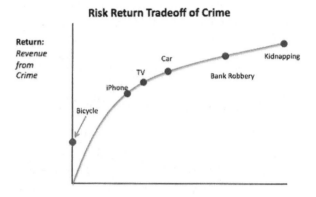

Risk to Criminal
Probability adjusted consequences of getting caught

Using this risk-return framework for crime, it begins to be clear why there is so much bike theft. For all practical purposes, stealing a bike is risk-free crime. It turns out there is a near zero chance you will be caught stealing a bike and if you are, the consequences are minimal.

Police officer Joe McKolsky of the San Francisco Police Department (SFPD) tells one journalist whose bike is stolen:

> *"We make it easy for them. The DA doesn't do tough prosecutions. All the thieves we've busted have got probation. They treat it like a petty crime. You can't take six people off a murder to investigate a bike theft."*

Bike thievery is essentially a risk-free crime, according to the police officer responsible for preventing bike theft in San Francisco. If you were a criminal, that might just strike your fancy. If Goldman Sachs didn't have more profitable market inefficiencies to exploit, they might be out there arbitraging stolen bikes.

What Happens to the Stolen Bikes?

Just because the risk of a crime is zero, that doesn't mean that a criminal will engage in that crime. If that were the case, thieves would go about stealing dandelions and day-old newspapers. There has to be customer demand and a liquid market for the product in order for the criminal to turn their contraband into revenue. So, how exactly does a criminal go about converting a stolen bicycle to cash?

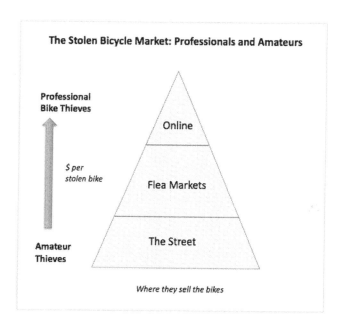

Amateur Bike Thieves

Amateur bike thieves sell their stolen goods at local fencing spots and are typically drug addicts or down on their luck homeless.

Sgt. Joe McKolsky of the SFPD estimates that the overwhelming majority of bike thefts are driven by drug addicts who sell stolen bikes on the street for 5 to 10 cents on the dollar. Any bike will do, whether it's a $50 beater or a $2,000 road bike. These thieves are amateurs just opportunistically stealing unsecured bikes to get some quick cash. Victor Veysey, a longtime San Francisco bike mechanic and messenger observes:

> *"Bikes are one of the four commodities of the street: cash, drugs, sex, and bikes...you can virtually exchange one for another."*

In San Francisco, these stolen bikes end up on the street at the intersection of 7th Street and Market Street in front of the Carl's Jr restaurant. We chatted with Brian Smith, co-owner of HuckleBerry Bicycles, which is located across the street from this fencing joint. He confirmed it's fairly common for people to come into the shop having just purchased a $50 bike across the street or with obviously stolen bikes they're trying to sell.

Professional Thieves

On the other end of the spectrum are professional bike thieves. Instead of opportunistically targeting poorly locked bicycles, these thieves target expensive bicycles. They have the tools that can cut through u-locks and aim to resell stolen bikes at a price near their "fair market value." These thieves acquire the bicycles from the streets, but then resell them on online markets to maximize the selling price.

We asked Aubrey Hoermann, owner of used bicycle shop Refried Cycles in the Mission, about professional bike thieves and where they sell their merchandise:

> *"It has to end up somewhere where you can sell it in another city. My feeling is that people steal enough bikes to make it worth taking a trip to somewhere like LA and then sell it there on Craigslist. If you have about 10 stolen bikes, it's probably worth the trip."*

Another bike shop proprietor who asked not to be named added:

> *"Most of these guys are drug addicts, but a lot of them are professionals. You can cut through a u-lock in a minute and a half with the right tools. Steal three bikes and sell them in LA for $1500 a piece and you're making money."*

These thieves essentially are maximizing their revenue per van trip to a market in which they can sell the bicycle. In the past they might've been able to resell it locally, but according to Aubrey Hoermann, this opportunity is fading:

> *"You can't just steal a bike and sell it on Craigslist in San Francisco anymore. It's too well known that that's where it would be and it's too much work to change it to make it look different. I used to be a bike messenger and if your bike was stolen you'd go check at 7th and Market. Now that's too well known to just sell a bike."*

Increasingly when a bicycle is stolen, the victims know where to check locally (Craigslist, 7th and Market, or the Oakland Flea Market if your bike is stolen in the Bay Area) so that makes it hard to sell the bikes there. Because bikes aren't even that popular in the first place, it's just not worth the effort to customize and disguise them for local sale.

Because of this dynamic, Hoermann concludes that professional bike theft is replacing amateur theft as the predominant form of bike theft. While the police may not penalize bicycle thieves, it's becoming easier for the person whose bike was stolen to investigate the bike theft themselves. This is making it harder for the amateur thief to casually flip a stolen bike.

Is There at Keyser Söze of the Bike Underworld?

Bike theft is rampant and increasingly the province of professionals. Is there any evidence that a "criminal mastermind" exists behind this network where bikes are stolen in one city, transported to another and then resold? Ultimately, there is no evidence that a bike kingpin exists.

The largest bike theft arrests ever recorded are rather mundane actually. In San Francisco, recently a local teen was arrested with hundreds of stolen bikes found in his storage locker. Did these bicycles end up in some exotic fencing ring? Nope. They were being resold at an Oakland flea market.

In Toronto, a mentally imbalanced bike shop owner was found hoarding 2,700 stolen bikes. Mostly, he was just letting them rust.

Criminal masterminds have to value their time and resources, and bike theft isn't really that profitable. The transportation costs and low value density ratio (bikes take up a lot of space in a transport van) of the product likely kill the economics of the stolen bike trade. The bike shop proprietor we interviewed (who requested anonymity) concluded:

> *"You'd be in the prostitution or drugs business if you were running a criminal ring to make money. There just isn't that much money in bikes. These people who steal bikes are professionals but small time operators. Or, they're just assholes."*

***

Ultimately, that's the point everyone seems to agree on — bike thieves are assholes. For everything else there is little consensus, though a few factors explain why bike theft occurs so often.

It's dead simple to steal a bike and the consequences are near zero. You can resell stolen bikes, but if you want to get a good price for a stolen bicycle, it requires a decent amount of work. That amount of work is what limits the bike theft trade from really flourishing. Criminal masterminds have an opportunity cost for their time; they can't be messing around lugging heavy pieces of metal and rubber that are only in limited demand.

So, if your bike ever gets stolen, you can at least take solace in the fact that the illicit bike trade isn't a very easy way to make a lot of money. That probably won't make you feel any better though.

CITATIONS

Introduction: The Big Lie

Big Lie (Wikipedia): http://en.wikipedia.org/wiki/Big_lie

The Big Lie (Wikipedia): http://en.wikipedia.org/wiki/The_Big_Lie

Part I: Status Symbols

Diamonds Are Bullshit

Intrinsic value (finance) – Wikipedia: http://en.wikipedia.org/wiki/Intrinsic_value_(finance)

Gold as an investment – Wikipedia: http://en.wikipedia.org/wiki/Gold_as_an_investment

How to Invest in Gold - The Street: http://www.thestreet.com/story/10389829/1/how-to-invest-in-gold.html

"Top 10 Retail Markups" – HowStuffWorks: http://money.howstuffworks.com/personal-finance/budgeting/5-retail-markups.htm#page=2

Diamonds as an investment – Wikipedia: http://en.wikipedia.org/wiki/Diamonds_as_an_investment

Have You Ever Tried to Sell a Diamond? - The Atlantic: http://www.theatlantic.com/magazine/archive/1982/02/have-you-ever-tried-to-sell-a-diamond/304575/

N. W. Ayer & Son - Wikipedia: http://en.wikipedia.org/wiki/N._W._Ayer_%26_Son

Engagement rings: good or bad? - Slate: http://www.slate.com/articles/news_and_politics/weddings/2007/06/diamonds_are_a_girls_worst_friend.html

Cecil Rhodes - Wikipedia: http://en.wikipedia.org/wiki/Cecil_Rhodes

De Beers - Wikipedia: http://en.wikipedia.org/wiki/De_Beers

The De Beers Story (CNN): http://money.cnn.com/magazines/fortune/fortune_archive/2001/02/19/296863/index.htm

Campaign group pulls out of 'blood diamond' scheme - CNN: http://www.cnn.com/2011/12/05/world/africa/south-africa-blood-diamonds

Diamonds: Betting on De Beers - The Economist: http://www.economist.-com/node/21538145

Jack Donaghy 20 Life Lessons - ETonline: http://www.etonline.com/daily-first/129834_Jack_Donaghy_20_Life_Lessons/index.html

Blood diamond - Wikipedia: http://en.wikipedia.org/wiki/Blood_diamond

The Seal Clubbing Business

Seal Timeline (Canadian Geographic):
http://www.canadiangeographic.ca/magazine/jf00/sealtimeline.asp

Death on the Ice (CBC News):
http://www.cbc.ca/news/canada/newfoundland-labrador/furlong-death-on-the-ice-time-to-pull-the-plug-on-the-seal-hunt-1.1154606

China Gives Canada Its Approval (The Star):
http://www.thestar.com/news/world/2010/01/13/china_gives_canada_its_approval_of_seal.html

Q+A (Fisheries and Oceans Canada):
http://www.dfo-mpo.gc.ca/media/back-fiche/2011/2011-01-12-eng.html

Films and Documentaries (ACPIM):
http://www.chasseursdephoques.com/movies.html

Terry Audla (The Huffington Post):
http://webcache.googleusercontent.com/search?q=cache:http://www.huff-ingtonpost.ca/terry-audla/sealing_b_5214956.html

Seat Hunt (Liberation BC): http://liberationbc.org/issues/seal_hunt

Always In Vogue: https://www.facebook.com/groups/94115954892/

Seal Harvest: http://www.sealharvest.ca/site/?page_id=1587

Veteran Seal Hunter Tells His Experiences (PEI Canada):
http://peicanada.com/past_alan_macrae/columns_opinions/veteran_seal_hunter_tells_his_experiences_william_case_sailed_newf

Seal Skin Ban (Urban Native): http://urbannativemag.com/sealskinban/

Seal Hunter Takes Aim At Ellen (Business Insider):
http://www.businessinsider.com/seal-hunters-ellen-degeneres-selfie-2014-4#ixzz34STjZlxQ

Humane Society Says It Doesn't Oppose Inuit Hunt (CBC News):
http://www.cbc.ca/news/canada/north/humane-society-says-it-doesn-t-

oppose-inuit-seal-hunt-1.2603306

Seal Pelt Market Softer (The Telegram):
http://www.thetelegram.com/News/Local/2014-04-21/article-
3696342/Seal-pelt-market-softer,-ice-conditions-harder%3A-sealer/1

Sealers Testimony (Global Action Network):
http://www.gan.ca/media/factsheets/index.en.html

Activists rally in Halifax... (Metro News):
http://metronews.ca/news/halifax/972962/activists-rally-in-halifax-to-
call-for-an-end-to-canadas-commercial-seal-hunt/

20,000 Species Are Near Extinction (National Geographic):
http://news.nationalgeographic.com/news/2013/12/131216-conservation-
environment-animals-science-endangered-species/

Canada Aims to Ease Whale Protection (Reuters):
http://www.reuters.com/article/2014/04/22/us-environment-whales-
idUSBREA3L1ZI20140422

Why is Art Expensive?

Lawsuits Claim Knoedler Made Huge Profits on Fakes (New York Times):
http://www.nytimes.com/2012/10/22/arts/design/knoedler-made-huge-
profits-on-fake-rothko-lawsuit-claims.html

Art Dealer Admits to Role in Fraud (New York Times): http://www.ny-
times.com/2013/09/17/arts/design/art-dealer-admits-role-in-selling-fake-
works.html

Christie's $745 Million Contemporary Art Sale is Most Expensive Single
Auction in History (Gallerist): http://galleristny.com/2014/05/christies-
745-million-contemporary-art-sale-is-most-expensive-single-auction-in-
history/

The Supermodel and the Brillo Box (Don Thompson): http://books.-
google.com/books/about/The_Supermodel_and_the_Brillo_Box.html?
id=3wRtAwAAQBAJ

'The Supermodel and the Brillo Box', by Don Thompson (Financial Times):
http://www.ft.com/intl/cms/s/2/9644894c-e66a-11e3-9a20-00144fe-
abdc0.html#axzz33SV3fec0

artnet.com (Art Market Technology): http://artmarkettechnology.com/cate-
gory/directory/online-auctions-directory/

The (Auction) House Doesn't Always Win (New York Times):
http://www.nytimes.com/2014/01/16/arts/design/christies-and-sothebys-
woo-big-sellers-with-a-cut.html

Seven Days in the Art World (Sarah Thornton):
http://books.google.com/books/about/Seven_Days_in_the_Art_World.ht
ml?id=GAnseuV1PbkC

Why The Mona Lisa Stands Out (Intelligent Life): http://moreintelli-
gentlife.com/content/ideas/ian-leslie/overexposed-works-art

Mere Exposure, Reproduction, and the Impressionist Canon (James Cutting): http://www.researchgate.net/publication/237065501_Mere_expo-
sure_reproduction_and_the_Impressionist_canon

Rogue Urinals (The Economist):
http://www.economist.com/node/15766467

Mere Exposure to Bad Art (British Journal of Aesthetics): http://bjaesthet-
ics.oxfordjournals.org/content/53/2/139

High-end art is one of the most manipulated markets in the world (Quartz):
http://qz.com/103091/high-end-art-is-one-of-the-most-manipulated-mar-
kets-in-the-world/

The Top-Selling Living Artist (Wall Street Journal):
http://online.wsj.com/news/articles/SB100014240529702047818045772
67770169368462

As Art Values Rise, So Do Concerns About Market's Oversight (New York
Times): http://www.nytimes.com/2013/01/28/arts/design/as-art-market-
rise-so-do-questions-of-oversight.html

How to Charge $1,000 for Absolutely Nothing

iReview, I Am Rich (iReviewApps99):
https://www.youtube.com/watch?v=G6oOLcdajXo

Apple Removes Featureless iPhone Application (LA Times):
http://latimesblogs.latimes.com/technology/2008/08/iphone-i-am-
ric.html

Guy Buys $999 I'm Rich App... (Gizmodo):
http://gizmodo.com/5034122/guy-buys-999-im-rich-app-discovers-hes-
just-dumb

Who Would Pay $1,000 for an iPhone Application? (ABC News):
http://abcnews.go.com/blogs/technology/2008/08/who-would-pay-1/

Is Wine Bullshit?

Does All Wine Taste the Same? - The New Yorker: http://www.newyorker.-
com/online/blogs/frontal-cortex/2012/06/wine-taste.html

Why Wine Ratings Are Badly Flawed - WSJ.com: http://online.wsj.com/article/SB10001424052748703683804574533840282653628.html

Wine tasting is bullshit. Here's why: http://io9.com/wine-tasting-is-bull-shit-heres-why-496098276

Watch What Happens When Wine "Connoisseurs" Are Given the Same Glass Of Wine Over and Over - PolicyMic: http://www.policymic.com/articles/50547/guess-what-happens-when-wine-connoisseurs-are-given-the-same-glass-of-wine-over-and-over

Taste - Wikipedia: http://en.wikipedia.org/wiki/Taste

Does The Way We See Food Affect Its Taste? (Huffington Post): http://www.huffingtonpost.com/Menuism/does-the-way-we-see-food-affect-taste_b_1872204.html

Can a food's brand affect your perceptions of taste? - Griffith Hack: http://www.griffithhack.com.au/mediacentre-Canafoodsbrandaffecty-ourperceptionsoftaste

Does a Price Tag Have a Taste? - Psychology Today: http://www.psychologytoday.com/blog/evolved-primate/201002/does-price-tag-have-taste

You Drink What You Think - Psychology Today: http://www.psychologytoday.com/blog/sensory-superpowers/200908/you-drink-what-you-think

Horsemeat Scandal Spreads to Ikea Swedish Meatballs - TIME.com: http://world.time.com/2013/02/26/horsemeat-scandal-spreads-to-ikea-swedish-meatballs/

The Billionaire's Vinegar (Benjamin Wallace): http://www.amazon.com/Billionaires-Vinegar-Mystery-Worlds-Expensive/dp/0307338789

Bordeaux 2011: http://www.decanter.com/bordeaux-2011/en-primeur-coverage/529916/bordeaux-2011-new-releases-but-lafite-dominating-early-sales-say-merchants

Select Bordeaux: http://www.selectbordeaux.com/newscontent.php?nid=25%20

Do More Expensive Wines Taste Better? (Freakonomics): http://www.freakonomics.com/2010/12/16/freakonomics-radio-do-more-expensive-wines-taste-better/"

What makes wine great? - Salon.com: http://www.salon.com/2010/06/02/how_soil_affects_wine_ext2010/

George Osumi, Cellar Employee, Allegedly Replaced $3 Million-Worth Of Wine With Trader Joe's Two Buck Chuck (Huffington Post): http://www.huffingtonpost.com/2012/10/11/george-osumi-wine-theft-two-buck-chuck_n_1958151.html

Discount Dynasty - SF Weekly: http://www.sfweekly.com/2005-08-24/news/discount-dynasty/full/%20

California, Wine; Rural Migration News - Migration Dialogue: http://migration.ucdavis.edu/rmn/more.php?id=826_0_5_0

Cheap Wine: Fred Franzia's Two Buck Chuck Turns Wine Industry On Its Head - ABC News: http://abcnews.go.com/Business/story?id=8311451&page=1#.UVXD-1sjqp0%20

Motorcycle Wineries: http://motorcyclewineries.com/

RESEARCH | Wine Market Council: http://winemarketcouncil.com/?page_id=35

[Yellow Tail] Tales (The Wine Economist): http://wineeconomist.com/2008/02/26/the-yellow-tail-tale/

The Million-Dollar Nose (The Atlantic): http://www.theatlantic.com/past/docs/issues/2000/12/langewiesche2.htm

Ten tips for successful investments in the wine market - GQ: http://www.gq-magazine.co.uk/comment/articles/2013-01/10/how-to-invest-in-wine-ten-tips/viewall

China surpasses one million millionaires - Financial Post: http://business.financialpost.com/2012/08/01/meet-the-average-chinese-millionaire-39-plays-golf-and-owns-an-ipad/

The Shadowy Residents of One Hyde Park - Vanity Fair: http://www.vanityfair.com/society/2013/04/mysterious-residents-one-hyde-park-london

Fine Wine 50: http://www.liv-ex.com/staticPageContent.do?pageKey=Fine_Wine_50

Lafite price comparison: Trade vs Auction - decanter.com: http://www.decanter.com/news/blogs/team/505083/lafite-price-comparison-trade-vs-auction

Welcome to Vinetrade: http://blog.vinetrade.com/2012/01/welcome-to-vinetrade/index.html

Liv-ex Fine Wine Market Blog: The Fine Wine Investment Market - An Inside View: http://www.blog.liv-ex.com/2011/11/the-fine-wine-investment-market-an-inside-view.html

Why Wine Ratings Are Badly Flawed - WSJ.com: http://online.wsj.com/article/SB10001424052748703683804574533840282653628.html

Does a Price Tag Have a Taste? - Psychology Today: http://www.psychologytoday.com/blog/evolved-primate/201002/does-price-tag-have-taste

Portfolio — sleepykyoto: http://sleepykyoto.com/portfolio/

Why Vinetrade Failed: http://jamesmaskell.co.uk/2013/why-vinetrade-failed/

PART II: Existing Power Structures

The Tyranny of Taxi Medallions

The Million-Dollar Taxi; Planet Money - NPR:
http://www.npr.org/blogs/money/2011/10/20/141546717/the-million-dollar-taxi

Essentials of Economics (Paul Krugman, Robin Wells, Kathryn Graddy):
http://books.google.com/books?
id=VXpyNs5EaHEC&pg=PA119&lpg=PA119&dq=taxi+medallion+economics&source=bl&ots=uJJmmmmZsi&sig=gLzqx7oq1UaUrYPhmoHGBM-gO1hc&hl=en&sa=X&ei=ioJlUYm5Mo_liwKe9IGQCQ&ved=0CC0Q6AE-wAA#v=onepage&q=taxi%20medallion%20economics&f=false

Taxicabs of New York City - Wikipedia: http://en.wikipedia.org/wiki/Taxicabs_of_New_York_City#1930s_.E2.80.93_Medallion_system_introduced

Medallion Sale Information - Background Information: http://www.nyc.gov/html/tlc/medallion/html/background/main.shtml

NYC Taxi & Limousine Commission - Average Medallion Price:
http://www.nyc.gov/html/tlc/html/about/average_medallion_price.shtml

Why taxi medallions cost $1 million - Felix Salmon: http://blogs.reuters.com/felix-salmon/2011/10/21/why-taxi-medallions-cost-1-million/

After 80 years of medallion oligopoly, Boston's taxi industry deserves something better - The Boston Globe:
http://www.bostonglobe.com/opinion/2013/04/06/after-years-medallion-oligopoly-boston-taxi-industry-deserves-something-better/6zposFZeNR-wmqCIVagZ9EJ/story.html

Plan lets taxi drivers transfer medallions - SFGate:
http://www.sfgate.com/bayarea/article/Plan-lets-taxi-drivers-transfer-medallions-3805587.php

Spotlight report - The Boston Globe:
http://www.bostonglobe.com/metro/2013/04/01/spotlight/IkU7kjxSy2d1N8eYhDTBaL/story.html

How many Taxi drivers and chauffeurs die per year?: http://dangerous-jobs.findthedata.org/q/38/1068/How-many-Taxi-drivers-and-chauffeurs-die-per-year

Ride-share services run into fines, suit - SFGate: http://www.sfgate.com/news/article/Ride-share-services-run-into-fines-suit-4048980.php

Uber: http://uber.com
Sidecar: http://www.side.cr/

Lyft: http://www.lyft.me/

InstaCab: http://instantcab.com

Being Really, Really, Ridiculously Good Looking

Beauty in the Victorian age - beautifulwithbrains.com: http://beautiful-withbrains.com/2010/08/06/beauty-in-the-victorian-age/

Perception abstract: http://www.perceptionweb.com/abstract.cgi?id=p3123

Halo effect - Wikipedia: http://en.wikipedia.org/wiki/Halo_effect

Influence: The Psychology of Persuasion (Collins Business Essentials): Robert B., PhD Cialdini: 9780061241895: Amazon.com: Books: http://www.amazon.com/Influence-Psychology-Persuasion-Business-Essentials/dp/006124189X

Fantastic Vintage Beer Ads | webexpedition18: http://webexpedition18.com/articles/fantastic-vintage-beer-ads/

Beautiful women face discrimination in certain jobs, study finds — ScienceDaily: http://www.sciencedaily.com/releases/2010/08/100806132218.htm

The absurd life of an Abercrombie & Fitch model - Salon.com: http://www.salon.com/2012/02/04/the_absurd_life_of_an_abercrombie_fitch_model/

Going for the Look, but Risking Discrimination - New York Times: http://www.nytimes.com/2003/07/13/us/going-for-the-look-but-risking-discrimination.html?pagewanted=all&src=pm

GS302 Cultural Studies; Semiotics and Political Economy Team analysis: http://blogs.stlawu.edu/chewculturalstudies/category/semiotics-and-political-economy-team-analysis/

History of Abercrombie & Fitch - Wikipedia: http://en.wikipedia.org/wiki/History_of_Abercrombie_%26_Fitch

Abercrombie & Fitch 4th-Quarter Profit Jumps on Revenue Growth - WSJ.com: http://online.wsj.com/article/BT-CO-20130222-705876.html

The Age Discrimination in Employment Act of 1967 (ADEA): http://www.eeoc.gov/laws/statutes/adea.cfm

A Guide to Disability Rights Laws: http://www.ada.gov/cguide.htm#anchor62335

Attractiveness discrimination: Hiring hotties - The Economist: http://www.economist.com/node/21559357

Men Sue Hooters for Sex Discrimination (UnderCover Waitress): http://www.undercoverwaitress.com/2012/03/men-sue-hooters-for-sex-discrimination.html#axzz2RV3eqzJN

Hot or Not - Wikipedia: http://en.wikipedia.org/wiki/Hot_or_Not

The Museum of Broadcast Communications - Encyclopedia of Television: http://www.museum.tv/eotvsection.php?entrycode=kennedy-nixon

The Ugly Truth About Beauty - ABC News: http://abcnews.go.com/2020/story?id=123853&page=2#.UXhy8isjqp0

Do Elite Colleges Discriminate Against Asians?

Stanford Magazine: http://alumni.stanford.edu/get/page/magazine/article/?article_id=32005
Ivies, Stanford, MIT post record-low admit rates - Cross Campus: http://yaledailynews.com/crosscampus/2013/03/29/ivies-stanford-mit-post-record-low-admit-rates/

Some Asians' college strategy: Don't check box – USATODAY.com: http://usatoday30.usatoday.com/news/education/story/2011-12-03/asian-students-college-applications/51620236/1

No Longer Separate, Not Yet Equal (Thomas J. Espenshade, Alexandria Walton Radford): http://www.amazon.com/Longer-Separate-Not-Yet-Equal/dp/0691141606

The Myth of American Meritocracy - The American Conservative: http://www.theamericanconservative.com/articles/the-myth-of-american-meritocracy/

Harvard Shuns Quotas and Narrow Criteria - NYTimes.com: http://www.nytimes.com/roomfordebate/2012/12/19/fears-of-an-asian-quota-in-the-ivy-league/harvard-shuns-quotas-and-narrow-criteria

Scores Aren't the Only Qualification - NYTimes.com: http://www.nytimes.com/roomfordebate/2012/12/19/fears-of-an-asian-quota-in-the-ivy-league/scores-arent-the-only-qualification

Asian-American Quotas Are Imaginary: http://www.nytimes.com/room-fordebate/2012/12/19/fears-of-an-asian-quota-in-the-ivy-league/asian-american-quotas-are-imaginary-need-for-diversity-is-real

Numerus clausus - Wikipedia:
http://en.wikipedia.org/wiki/Numerus_clausus#Numerus_clausus_in_the_United_States

Da Da Da Da Life Goes On; December 2011:
http://dcmcd2.blogspot.com/2011_12_01_archive.html

The Industrial Food Complex

Mondelez International Fact Sheet (Mondelez International):
http://www.mondelezinternational.com/investors

Pepsico Inc (Bloomberg):
http://investing.businessweek.com/research/stocks/earnings/earn-ings.asp?ticker=PEP

Kellogg Co (Bloomberg):
http://investing.businessweek.com/research/stocks/earnings/earn-ings.asp?ticker=K

Fruit and Vegetable Backgrounder (U.S. Department of Agriculture Economic Research Service):
http://www.ers.usda.gov/publications/vgs-vegetables-and-pulses-outlook/vgs-31301.aspx#.U58ak5RdXgJ

Ketchup is a Vegetable? Again? (The Atlantic):
http://www.theatlantic.com/health/archive/2011/11/ketchup-is-a-veg-etable-again/248538/

School Lunch Proposals Set Off A Dispute (The New York Times):
http://www.nytimes.com/2011/11/02/us/school-lunch-proposals-set-off-a-dispute.html

Pizza Is Not A Vegetable (Slate):
http://www.slate.com/articles/life/food/2011/11/pizza_ruling_in_con-gress_what_is_a_vegetable_really_.html

No, Congress Did Not Declare Pizza A Vegetable (Washington Post):
http://www.washingtonpost.com/blogs/wonkblog/post/did-congress-de-clare-pizza-as-a-vegetable-not-exactly/2011/11/20/gIQABXgmhN_blog.html

ConAgra Sales Jump, But Weakness Still Prevalent (Market Watch):
http://www.marketwatch.com/story/conagra-sales-jump-but-weakness-still-prevalent-2014-03-20

Private Companies — Top 25 (Twin Cities Business):
http://tcbmag.com/Lists-and-Research/BIG-Book?
djoPage=view_html&djoPid=18844

Food Processing and Sales (Open Secrets):
http://www.opensecrets.org/lobby/indusclient.php?id=A09

Vegetables and Fruits (Open Secrets):
http://www.opensecrets.org/industries/indus.php?ind=A1400

Cereal Killers: Americans' New Breakfast Habits (CNBC):
http://www.cnbc.com/id/100983729

U.S. Farm Income (Congressional Research Service):
http://digitalcommons.ilr.cornell.edu/key_workplace/1167/

40 Maps That Explain Food in America (Vox Media):
http://www.vox.com/a/explain-food-america

Drop That Spoon! The Truth About Breakfast Cereals (The Guardian):
http://www.theguardian.com/business/2010/nov/23/food-book-extract-fe-
licity-lawrence

2013 Annual Report (Kellog's):
http://investor.kelloggs.com/investor-relations/annual-reports/default-
.aspx

Kellogg Co Stock Quote (Bloomberg):
http://www.bloomberg.com/quote/K:US

Why Are Honeycrisp Apples So Damn Expensive? (Esquire):
http://www.esquire.com/blogs/food-for-men/honeycrisp-price-explained

The Cost of Kale: How Foodie Trends Can Hurt Low-Income Families (Bitch
Magazine):
http://bitchmagazine.org/post/the-cost-of-kale-how-foodie-trends-can-
hurt-low-income-families

Fresh Fruit and Vegetable Marketing and Trade Information (UC Davis
Agricultural & Resource Economics):
http://agecon.ucdavis.edu/people/faculty/roberta-cook/docs/articles.php

Vegetables and Pulses Overview (U.S. Department of Agriculture Economic
Research Service):
http://www.ers.usda.gov/topics/crops/vegetables-pulses.aspx#.U6C-
QdZRdVCN

Financial Characteristics of Vegetable and Melon Farms (U.S. Department
of Agriculture Economic Research Service):
http://books.google.com/books/about/Financial_Characteristics_of_Veg-

etable_a.html?id=VdnfNAEACAAJ

The Extraordinary Science of Addictive Junk Food (New York Times Magazine):
http://www.nytimes.com/2013/02/24/magazine/the-extraordinary-science-of-junk-food.html

Eating Well (New York Times):
http://www.nytimes.com/1992/07/01/garden/eating-well.html

Food Politics (University of California Press):
http://books.google.com/books/about/Food_Politics.html?id=zvzTIU-V9XNwC

Taxpayers Turn U.S. Farmers Into Fat Cats With Subsidies (Bloomberg):
http://www.bloomberg.com/news/2013-09-09/farmers-boost-revenue-sowing-subsidies-for-crop-insurance.html

Pharma, Utilities and Big Ag Lead Lobbying in 2012 (Open Secrets):
https://www.opensecrets.org/news/2012/04/pharma-utilities-and-big-ag-lead-lo/

Farmer In Chief (New York Times Magazine):
http://www.nytimes.com/2008/10/12/magazine/12policy-t.html

Our Daily Bread (Boston Review):
http://www.bostonreview.net/rosamond-naylor-and-walter-falcon-our-daily-bread-global-food-crisis

The Farm Bill: From Charitable Start to Prime Budget Target (NPR):
http://www.npr.org/blogs/thesalt/2011/09/26/140802243/the-farm-bill-from-charitable-start-to-prime-budget-target

Plowing Farm Subsidies Under (National Review):
http://www.nationalreview.com/articles/220948/plowing-farm-subsidies-under/bruce-gardner

A Fatally Flawed Food Guide (Whale): http://www.whale.to/a/light.html

Expect A Food Fight as U.S. Sets to Revise Diet Guidelines (Wall Street Journal):
http://online.wsj.com/news/articles/SB10602937393859600

Why is Science Behind a Paywall?

UC research should be free - The Daily Californian: http://www.dailycal.org/2013/02/01/uc-research-should-be-free/

Standing on the shoulders of giants - Wikipedia:
http://en.wikipedia.org/wiki/Standing_on_the_shoulders_of_giants

Leibniz–Newton calculus controversy - Wikipedia:
http://en.wikipedia.org/wiki/Leibniz%E2%80%93Newton_calculus_controversy

Open science - Wikipedia: http://en.wikipedia.org/wiki/Open_science

The Future of Science - Michael Nielsen:
http://michaelnielsen.org/blog/the-future-of-science-2/

File:1665 phil trans vol i title.png - Wikipedia:
http://en.wikipedia.org/wiki/File:1665_phil_trans_vol_i_title.png

Faculty Advisory Council Memorandum on Journal Pricing (THE HARVARD LIBRARY): http://isites.harvard.edu/icb/icb.do?
keyword=k77982&tabgroupid=icb.tabgroup143448

Elsevier: http://www.elsevier.com/

Digital Marketing & Design Agency based in Central London - SAS:
http://reporting.reedelsevier.com/media/174016/reed_elsevier_ar_2012.pdf

The Business of Academic Publishing: http://southernlibrarianship.icaap.org/content/v09n03/mcguigan_g01.html

Is the Academic Publishing Industry on the Verge of Disruption? - US News:
http://www.usnews.com/news/articles/2012/07/23/is-the-academic-publishing-industry-on-the-verge-of-disruption

Exclusion or efficient pricing? The "big deal" bundling of academic journals
(eScholarship): http://escholarship.org/uc/item/3nd7v77z#page-4

A message to the research community: Journal prices, discounts and access
- Elsevier: http://www.elsevier.com/about/issues-and-information/elsevieropenletter

Publishing, perishing, and peer review - The Economist: http://www.economist.com/node/603719

Publications | PLOS: http://www.plos.org/publications/

Researchers Finally Replicated Reinhart-Rogoff, and There Are Serious
Problems - Next New Deal: http://www.nextnewdeal.net/rortybomb/researchers-finally-replicated-reinhart-rogoff-and-there-are-serious-problems

Reinhart-Rogoff Rebuttal Says UMass Critics Politicized Debt - Bloomberg:
http://www.bloomberg.com/news/2013-04-26/reinhart-rogoff-dispute-umass-criticism-of-debt-study-findings.html"

Peer review is f***ed up – let's fix it: http://www.michaeleisen.org/blog/?p=694

GitHub; Build software better, together: https://github.com/

Tim Berners-Lee- Wikipedia: http://en.wikipedia.org/wiki/Tim_Berners-Lee

Is College Worth It?

College Education Value Rankings - PayScale 2013 College ROI Report
: http://www.payscale.com/college-education-value-2013"
Where is the Best Place to Invest $102,000 — The Hamilton Project:
http://www.hamiltonproject.org/papers/where_is_the_best_place_to_inv
est_102000_--_in_stocks_bonds_or_a_colle/%20

20 Surprising Higher Education Facts - US News:
http://www.usnews.com/education/blogs/the-college-solution/2011/09/06/20-surprising-higher-education-facts

9 Problems with Payscale.com's College Rankings (and One Solution) -
Around Learning: http://aroundlearning.com/2013/09/8-problems-with-payscale-coms-college-rankings-and-one-solution/
College Scorecard:
http://collegecost.ed.gov/scorecard/UniversityProfile.aspx?
org=s&id=243744"

Shocking Chart on Tuition vs. Earnings for College Grads - The Fiscal
Times: http://www.thefiscaltimes.com/Articles/2012/11/30/Shocking-Chart-on-Tuition-vs-Earnings-for-College-Grads#page1%20

What's Really 'Immoral' About Student Loans - WSJ.com: http://on-line.wsj.com/article/SB10001424127887324688404578541372861440606.
html?mod=WSJ_article_comments#articleTabs%3Darticle
Regardless of the Cost, College Still Matters - Brookings Institution:
http://www.brookings.edu/blogs/jobs/posts/2012/10/05-jobs-greenstone-looney"

The Tuition is Too Damn High, Part II; Why college is still worth it:
http://www.washingtonpost.com/blogs/wonkblog/wp/2013/08/27/the-tuition-is-too-damn-high-part-ii-why-college-is-still-worth-it/

How Art History Majors Power the U.S. Economy - Bloomberg View:
http://www.bloomberg.com/news/2012-01-06/postrel-how-art-history-majors-power-the-u-s-.html

Academically Adrift (Richard Arum, Josipa Roksa):
http://www.amazon.com/Academically-Adrift-Limited-Learning-Campuses/dp/0226028550

Public Universities Ramp Up Aid for the Wealthy, Leaving the Poor Behind -
ProPublica: http://www.propublica.org/article/how-state-schools-ramp-up-aid-for-the-wealthy-leaving-the-poor-behind

The Scariest Student Loan Figure is $14,500 - NewAmerica.org:
http://higheredwatch.newamerica.net/blogposts/2013/debt_dollars_need
_context-89338

Welcome to CollegeMeasures.org - CollegeMeasures.org: http://college-
measures.org/4-year_colleges/home/

Why Do You Think They're Called For-Profit Colleges? - The Chronicle of
Higher Education: http://chronicle.com/article/Why-Do-You-Think-
Theyre/123660/

Annual Portrait of Education Documents Swift Rise of For-Profit Colleges -
The Chronicle of Higher Education:
http://chronicle.com/article/Annual-Portrait-of-Education/127639/

Bankers Warn Fed of Farm, Student Loan Bubbles Echoing Subprime -
Businessweek: http://www.businessweek.com/news/2013-05-07/bankers-
warn-fed-of-farm-student-loan-bubbles-echoing-subprime%20

NY Fed: Student Loans Presentation - Business Insider: http://www.busi-
nessinsider.com/ny-fed-student-loans-presentation-2013-2#people-with-
lots-of-student-debt-are-less-likely-to-take-out-a-mortgage-15

Massive open online course - Wikipedia:
http://en.wikipedia.org/wiki/Massive_open_online_course

Rohan Dixit: http://www.rohandixit.com

Josh Freedman - Forbes: http://www.forbes.com/sites/joshfreedman/

College ROI 2013 Methodology: http://www.payscale.com/data-
packages/college-roi-2013/methodology"

IPEDS Data Center: http://nces.ed.gov/ipeds/datacenter/Default.aspx"

College Scorecard: http://collegecost.ed.gov/scorecard/"

FinAid Calculators - Education Loan Interest Rates:
http://www.finaid.org/loans/scripts/interest.cgi

Is College Worth It? (FiveThirtyEight):
http://fivethirtyeight.com/datalab/is-college-worth-it-it-depends-on-
whether-you-graduate/

The Class of 2011: Young Workers Face a Dire Labor Market Without a
Safety Net (Economic Policy Institute):
http://www.epi.org/publication/bp306-class-of-2011/

PART III: The Business of Manipulation

How Marketers Invented Body Odor

Genetically, Some of Us Never Have Body Odor, But We Still Think We're Smelly - Motherboard: http://motherboard.vice.com/blog/even-if-you-dont-smell-you-probably-use-deodorant

The Power of Habit by Charles Duhigg: http://charlesduhigg.com/the-power-of-habit/

History, Travel, Arts, Science, People, Places - Smithsonian: http://www.-smithsonianmag.com/history-archaeology/How-Advertisers-Convinced-Americans-They-Smelled-Bad-164779646.html?c=y&story=fullstory

AAF Hall of Fame: Members: http://advertisinghall.org/members/member_bio.php?memid=826

The World's Most Expensive Free Credit Report

Marketer of Free Credit Reports Settles FTC Charges (FTC): http://www.ftc.gov/news-events/press-releases/2005/08/marketer-free-credit-reports-settles-ftc-charges

Consumerinfo.com Settles FTC Charges (FTC): http://www.ftc.gov/news-events/press-releases/2007/02/consumerinfo-com-settles-ftc-charges

False Advertising (Wikipedia): http://en.wikipedia.org/wiki/False_advertising

Snapchat and FTC Privacy and Security Consent Orders (LinkedIn): https://www.linkedin.com/today/post/article/20140512053224-2259773-the-anatomy-of-an-ftc-privacy-and-data-security-consent-order

FTC Finally Forces FreeCreditReport.com To Be Honest (Tech Dirt): https://www.techdirt.com/articles/20100302/2343298378.shtml

Queen's birthday honours list - Knights (The Guardian) http://www.theguardian.com/uk/2011/jun/11/queens-birthday-honours-knights

Credit Card Act of 2009 (Wikipedia): http://en.wikipedia.org/wiki/Credit_CARD_Act_of_2009

AnnualCreditReport.com: https://www.annualcreditreport.com/index.action

Credit checker Experian fears Brazil World Cup toll on business (Financial Times):

http://www.ft.com/intl/cms/s/0/ebd8bbb6-d5c2-11e3-a017-00144fe-abdc0.html#axzz33n9Q6oex

FreeCreditScore.com (Wikipedia):
http://en.wikipedia.org/wiki/FreeCreditScore.com

What Happens to Donated Cars?

Most Expensive Keywords in Google (Fetch123):
http://www.fetch123.com/SEM/the-most-expensive-keywords-in-google

Vehicle Donations (US General Accounting Office):
http://www.gao.gov/new.items/d0473.pdf

Cars (Priceonomics)
http://priceonomics.com/cars/

Pennies for Charity (NY Attorney General):
http://www.charitiesnys.com/pdfs/2012_Pennies.pdf

Tips on Contributing Used Cars to Charity (BBB):
http://www.bbb.org/us/article/tips-on-contributing-used-cars-to-charity-458

Car Donation Contact (Carsfightingcancer.org):
http://www.carsfightingcancer.org/car-donation-contact.php

Cars (BBB Toledo):
http://toledo.bbb.org/article/bbb-urges-caution-on-others-first-car-dona-tion-programs-28610

Tax Form 990 (kars4kids.org):
http://www.kars4kids.org/charity/images/file-2010.pdf

Sham Car Donation Charity (NY Attorney General):
http://www.ag.ny.gov/press-release/attorney-general-cuomo-announces-arrest-and-guilty-plea-founder-sham-car-donation

The Invention of the Chilean Sea Bass

Blackened Chilean Seabass - Chef Just's Blog: http://chefjust.com/blog/?p=103

Aquacalypse Now - New Republic:
http://www.newrepublic.com/article/environment-energy/aquacalypse-now

Just how badly are we overfishing the oceans? (The Washington Post):
http://www.washingtonpost.com/blogs/wonkblog/wp/2013/10/29/just-how-badly-are-we-overfishing-the-ocean/0/%20

Unpopular, Unfamiliar Fish Species Suffer From Become Seafood:
http://www.washingtonpost.com/wp-
dyn/content/article/2009/07/30/AR2009073002478_2.html

Hooked (G. Bruce Knecht):
http://books.google.com/books/about/Hooked.html?id=kDE11cR-e8kC

Chasing the Perfect Fish (WSJ):
http://online.wsj.com/news/articles/SB114670694136643399

Restaurants remove toothfish from menus (USATODAY): http://usato-
day30.usatoday.com/news/science/cold-science/2002-02-19-toothfish.htm

The Encyclopedia of American Food and Drink - John F. Mariani:
http://books.google.com/books/about/The_Encyclopedia_of_American_F
ood_and_Dr.html?id=RQ2NAAAACAAJ

How the Lobster Clawed its Way Up - Mother Jones: http://www.mother-
jones.com/politics/2006/03/how-lobster-clawed-its-way

Atlantic Unbound:
https://www.theatlantic.com/past/docs/unbound/interviews/int2004-06-
30.htm

Chilean Sea Bass: More Than an Identity Problem - New York Times:
http://www.nytimes.com/2002/05/29/dining/chilean-sea-bass-more-
than-an-identity-problem.html

U.S. Chefs Join Campaign to Save Chilean Sea Bass: http://news.national-
geographic.com/news/2002/05/0522_020522_seabass.html

Unpopular, Unfamiliar Fish Species Suffer From Become Seafood:
http://www.washingtonpost.com/wp-
dyn/content/article/2009/07/30/AR2009073002478_2.html?

The Seafood List: http://www.accessdata.fda.gov/scripts/fdcc/?
set=seafoodlist&sort=SLSN&order=ASC&startrow=1&type=basic&search=t
oothfish

Chilean Seabass; Seafood Watch - Monterey Bay Aquarium:
http://www.seafoodwatch.org/cr/seafoodwatch/web/sfw_factsheet.aspx?
gid=11

PART IV: Suspension of Human Decency

What It's Like to Fail

Tell Me Something, She Said - David Raether: http://amzn.to/1f8qZ5N

How Many People Have Lost Their Homes? US Home Foreclosures are Comparable to the Great Depression - Global Research: http://www.global-research.ca/how-many-people-have-lost-their-homes-us-home-foreclo-sures-are-comparable-to-the-great-depression/5335430

2002–03 United States network television schedule - Wikipedia: http://en.wikipedia.org/wiki/2002%E2%80%9303_United_States_net-work_television_schedule

2007–08 United States network television schedule - Wikipedia: http://en.wikipedia.org/wiki/2007%E2%80%9308_United_States_net-work_television_schedule

Economist's View: Bad Advice from Experts, Herding, and Bubbles: http://economistsview.typepad.com/economistsview/2013/01/bad-advice-from-experts-herding-and-bubbles.html

1742 Warwick Rd, San Marino, CA 91108 - Redfin: http://www.redfin.com/CA/San-Marino/1742-Warwick-Rd-91108/home/7016580

Get Credit For Lifelong Learning - College, MOOCs & More: Degreed: http://degreed.com/

David Raether: http://www.davidraether.com/

How We Treat Pets in America

Donate to the ASPCA: http://www.aspca.org/about-us/faq/pet-statis-tics.aspx

Pet Industry Market Size & Ownership Statistics: http://www.american-petproducts.org/press_industrytrends.asp

Common Questions about Animal Shelters (The Humane Society of the United States): http://www.humanesociety.org/animal_community/re-sources/qa/common_questions_on_shelters.html#How_many_animals_e nter_animal_shelters_e

20 Sad Puppies That Will Ruin Your Day: http://www.buzzfeed.com/paws/sad-puppies-that-will-ruin-your-day? sub=1426726_134803

Pet Overpopulation: http://www.americanhumane.org/animals/adoption-pet-care/issues-information/pet-overpopulation.html

Animal Overpopulation: http://www.oxfordpets.com/index.php? option=com_content&view=article&id=61

Pet Health Library - AAHA: http://www.healthypet.com/PetCare/PetCareArticle.aspx?

title=Why_Do_Pets_End_Up_in_Shelters"
www.animalrescuesoc.org: http://www.animalrescuesoc.org/

Puppy mill - Wikipedia: http://en.wikipedia.org/wiki/Puppy_mill

More Than 100 Animals Rescued from Arkansas Puppy Mill - YouTube:
http://www.youtube.com/watch?v=C34ML7b_WuM

Investigating Puppy Mills: http://www.oprah.com/oprahshow/Investigat-
ing-Puppy-Mills/

Puppy Mills - SourceWatch: http://www.sourcewatch.org/index.php?
title=Puppy_mills

Audit of USDA Puppy Mill (Examiner):
http://www.examiner.com/article/audit-of-usda-puppy-mill-inspections-
finds-usda-ineffective-at-enforcing-the-animal-welfare-act

Kimberly K. Smith - PhilPapers: http://philpapers.org/rec/SMIAPC-2

Dog Cart, 19th Century Photograph by Granger:
http://fineartamerica.com/featured/dog-cart-19th-century-granger.html

Dog Days - Wikipedia: http://en.wikipedia.org/wiki/Dog_days

Pets in America: A History - Katherine C. Grier:
http://books.google.com/books?id=NNrlt_jPKHAC&q=%22dog+days
%22#v=snippet&q=%22dog%20days%22&f=false

About Us - ASPCA: http://www.aspca.org/about-us/history.aspx

Behind the big drop in euthanasia for America's dogs and cats - CSMoni-
tor.com: http://www.csmonitor.com/USA/Society/2012/0210/Behind-the-
big-drop-in-euthanasia-for-America-s-dogs-and-cats/(page)/2

Animal Sheltering Trends in the U.S. : The Humane Society of the United
States:
http://www.humanesociety.org/animal_community/resources/timelines/a
nimal_sheltering_trends.html

Evicted in San Francisco

Listing 417171; San Francisco 2-4 Unit Building For Sale: http://vanguards-
f.com/MFM2-417171.php

San Francisco likely has tens of thousands of people living under the stairs -
Examiner: http://www.sfexaminer.com/sanfrancisco/san-francisco-likely-
has-tens-of-thousands-of-people-living-under-the-stairs/Content?
oid=2337031

S.F. in-law proposal would make units legal (SFGate): http://www.sfgate.-

com/bayarea/article/S-F-in-law-proposal-would-make-units-legal-5011267.php

Department of Building Inspection: http://dbiweb.sfgov.org/dbipts/default.aspx?page=AddressComplaint&ComplaintNo=201175835

Housing, Community & Services for LGBT Seniors - Openhouse: http://openhouse-sf.org/

San Francisco Rent Board : Section 37.9 Evictions: http://www.sfrb.org/index.aspx?page=1261

San Francisco Tenants Union: http://www.sftu.org/eviction.html

Department of Building Inspection: http://dbiweb.sfgov.org/dbipts/default.aspx?page=PermitDetails

The Law Offices of Bornstein & Bornstein in San Francisco: http://www.yelp.com/biz_photos/bornstein-and-bornstein-san-francisco?select=6ME72c5t6yuDI781JFgOAQ#BOtWBPOCY0Mh8iXHGNrtMw"

Bornstein & Bornstein Law Offices: http://www.bornsteinandbornstein.com/

SF Law Firm Giving Landlords Free Workshops on How to Evict Tenants - 7x7: http://www.7x7.com/arts-culture/sf-law-firm-giving-landlords-free-workshops-how-evict-tenants

Lawyer pumps up S.F. landlords at boot camp - SFGate: http://www.sfgate.com/bayarea/article/Lawyer-pumps-up-S-F-landlords-at-boot-camp-5008552.php#page-2

Lawyer From "Eviction Boot Camp" Firm Fined, Reprimanded During Contentious Effort To Evict Outer Richmond Tenants: http://sfappeal.com/2014/02/lawyer-from-eviction-boot-camp-firm-fined-and-reprimanded-during-contentious-effort-to-evict-richmond-district-tenants/

Ellis Act Evictions - Anti-Eviction Mapping Project: http://www.antievictionmappingproject.net/ellis.html

Episcopal Community Services (ECS) of San Francisco: http://www.ecs-sf.org/

The McDonalds Monopoly Fraud

4 Sentenced in Scam That Rigged Contest - Los Angeles Times: http://articles.latimes.com/2003/jan/31/nation/na-mcdonalds31

McDonald's Monopoly is Back! - RedFlagDeals.com: http://www.redflagdeals.com/deal/fast-food/mcdonalds-monopoly-is-back-1-in-4-chances-to-win-food-prizes-gift-cards-vacations-and-more/

MONOPOLY Game at McDonald's Winners Gallery: http://winners.play-atmcd.com/

The Math Behind McDonald's Monopoly - Business Insider: http://www.businessinsider.com/math-mcdonalds-monopoly-odds-proba-bility-2013-7

Transcripts -CNN.com: http://transcripts.cnn.com/TRANSCRIPTS/0108/22/bp.00.html

Mastermind of McDonald's scam sentenced - Jacksonville.com: http://jacksonville.com/tu-online/stories/010903/met_11432178.shtml

Inmate Locator: http://www.bop.gov/inmateloc/

Man charged in McDonald's scam pleads guilty | Jacksonville.com: http://jacksonville.com/tu-online/stories/040502/met_mcdonalds.html %20

Woman Sues McDonald's For $2.2 Million over Monopoly Winnings - Chief Marketer: http://www.chiefmarketer.com/news/woman-sues-mcdonalds-for-2-2-million-over-monopoly-winnings-02062005"

Eight charged with defrauding McDonald's for prizes - chicagotribune.com: http://www.chicagotribune.com/sns-mcdonalds,0,6473748.story

McScam: FBI busts fast food game ring - Jacksonville.com: http://jack-sonville.com/tu-online/stories/082201/met_7010800.html

What Happens to Stolen Bicycles?

L.A. Sees Big Jump In Bike Thefts - Master Lock Street Cuffs: http://mas-terlocks.snipershots.net/street-cuffs-l-a-sees-big-jump-in-bike-thefts/

Stolen Bikes - OutsideOnline.com: http://www.outsideonline.com/outdoor-adventure/biking/Who-Pinched-My-Ride.html?page=2"

The Chicago Maroon — The economics of crime with Gary Becker: http://chicagomaroon.com/2012/05/25/the-economics-of-crime-with-gary-becker/

The New York Times: http://www.nytimes.com/2012/03/13/opinion/bike-thief.html?_r=1

Chasing my stolen bicycle - SF Bay Guardian: http://www.sfbg.com/2007/02/13/chasing-my-stolen-bicycle?page=0,1

National Bike Registry - College Students Beware!: http://www.national-bikeregistry.com/crime.html

Huckleberry Bicycles : http://www.huckleberrybicycles.com/

Index: http://refriedcycles.com/

The Usual Suspects final scene - YouTube: http://www.youtube.com/watch?v=D5k73jx2mIc&feature=fvwrel

Irving Morales-Sanchez Charged With Stealing Bikes - SF Weekly: http://blogs.sfweekly.com/thesnitch/2012/07/irving_morales-sanchezcraigslist_stolen_bikes.php

A Nice Place to Buy & Sell Bicycles - Racklove: https://racklove.com/?ref=blogpo"

ABOUT THE AUTHORS

Priceonomics is a San Francisco-based company that writes about data, business, and economics, and also provides data services for businesses. The authors of this book are:

Rohin Dhar *(CEO and founder)*
Rohin is a new dad. He likes to ride bikes and drink coffee. He holds an MBA from Stanford and BA from Dartmouth.

Zachary Crockett *(Writer)*
Zack plays many stringed instruments, climbs mountains, and is working on a collection of South American travel narratives.

Alex Mayyasi *(Writer)*
Alex enjoys hiking, good food, and the rare days when the San Francisco fog lifts. He is also writing a book about the Egyptian Revolution.

Everything Is Bullshit also features an essay by **David Raether** ("What It's Like To Fail"), and cover artwork b y **Dan Abramson**, a world-renowned designer of yoga mats that look like burritos.